REVOLUTION

CRITICAL
ANTIQUITIES
A SERIES EDITED BY BROOKE HOLMES & MARK PAYNE

Revolution

MODERN UPRISINGS
IN ANCIENT TIME

MIRIAM LEONARD

The University of Chicago Press
CHICAGO AND LONDON

An open access digital edition of this book is available thanks to
University College London.

The terms of the license for the open access digital edition are
Creative Commons Attribution-Non-Commercial-No-Derivatives 4.0
International License (CC BY-NC-ND 4.0). To view a copy of this license, visit
https://creativecommons.org/licenses/by-nc-nd/4.0/.

The University of Chicago Press, Chicago 60637
The University of Chicago Press, Ltd., London
© 2025 by The University of Chicago
Subject to the exception mentioned above, no part of this book may be used or reproduced in any manner whatsoever without written permission, except in the case of brief quotations in critical articles and reviews. For more information, contact the University of Chicago Press, 1427 E. 60th St., Chicago, IL 60637.
Published 2025

34 33 32 31 30 29 28 27 26 25   1 2 3 4 5

ISBN-13: 978-0-226-84303-2 (cloth)
ISBN-13: 978-0-226-84305-6 (paper)
ISBN-13: 978-0-226-84304-9 (ebook)
DOI: https://doi.org/10.7208/chicago/9780226843049.001.0001

Library of Congress Cataloging-in-Publication Data

Names: Leonard, Miriam, author.
Title: Revolution : modern uprisings in ancient time / Miriam Leonard.
Description: Chicago : The University of Chicago Press, 2025. | Series: Critical antiquities | Includes bibliographical references and index.
Identifiers: LCCN 2024061800 | ISBN 9780226843032 cloth | ISBN 9780226843056 paperback | ISBN 9780226843049 ebook
Subjects: LCSH: Revolutions—Philosophy | Social change—Philosophy | Civilization, Modern—Classical influences
Classification: LCC JC491 .L434 2025 | DDC 909.8—dc23/eng/20250311
LC record available at https://lccn.loc.gov/2024061800

FOR ISAAC

Contents

List of Illustrations	ix
Introduction	1
Time	17
Genre	46
Fraternity	79
Epilogue	107
Acknowledgments	113
Notes	115
Works Cited	127
Index	137

Illustrations

FIGURE 1   Jacques-Louis David, *The Death of Socrates*, 1787 · 6
FIGURE 2   Jacques-Louis David, *The Lictors Bring to Brutus the Bodies of His Sons*, 1789 · 15
FIGURE 3   Philibert-Louis Debucourt, *Calendrier républicain* (*Republican calendar*) · 23
FIGURE 4   *Frimaire* (November/December), third month of the Republican calendar · 28
FIGURE 5   Jacques-Louis David, *The Tennis Court Oath*, 1790–94 · 38
FIGURE 6   Jacques-Louis David, *The Intervention of the Sabine Women*, 1795–99 · 44
FIGURE 7   Jacques-Louis David, *The Oath of the Horatii*, 1784–85 · 80

Introduction

Revolution, as it is understood today, despite the term's Latin etymology, arguably did not exist in Greco-Roman antiquity.[1] There was certainly a history of momentous political change: from the "invention" of Greek democracy to the establishment of the Roman Republic, to its later transformation into imperial rule, and later still to the Christianization of the empire.[2] Political thinkers such as Plato, Aristotle, Cicero, and Polybius discussed the causes of political upheaval and even explained how one form of government could give way to another. But these thinkers mapped alternations in existing political constitutions rather than offering an account of transformation. For the Greeks and Romans, novelty tended to be troped negatively and innovation was often consciously inscribed into a narrative of political continuity rather than rupture.[3]

In fact, the ancient Greek and Roman understanding of historical change left its mark on the vocabulary of revolution well into the early modern period in Europe. The word *revolution* was originally used to describe natural phenomena rather than social or political uprisings, and it only gradually took on the connotation of a convulsive or irreversible moment of transformation. As the critic Steven Shapin argues, "The notion of revolution . . . was first applied in systematic ways to events in science and only later to political events. . . . The first revolutions may have been scientific, and the 'American,' 'French,' and 'Russian Revolutions' are its progeny."[4] The "Copernican Revolution" encapsulates some of the paradoxes of the term in the modern era. Taking its name from the title of Copernicus's treatise *De revolutionibus orbium coelestium*, here the phrase refers to the regular and circular movement of the heavenly bodies around the sun. Yet in the title of Thomas Kuhn's book *The Copernican Revolution*, the word *revolution* is chosen to signify the paradigm shift—that is to say, the convulsive and irreversible transformation in thought—that Copernicus's treatise exemplified. In her 1963 book *On Revolution*, Hannah Arendt argues that "revolutions, properly speaking, did not exist prior to the modern age; they are amongst the most recent of all political data."[5] Arendt establishes revolution as an inescapable "metaphor" of the modern condition. Modernity is characterized for political theorists such as Arendt by this new understanding of revolution: an understanding that insists on the incommensurability of antiquity and modernity.

The contemporary philosopher Tristan Garcia sees the modernity of revolution as a by-product of a more fundamental drive: the pursuit of intensity.

> For some centuries we have embodied a certain type of humanity: people shaped by the search, not for transcendence, as those of other epochs and cultures were, but for intensification. . . . Revolutionary heroism, regularly opposed to the market-oriented universe, was based on defending the intensity of "real life" against the self-centred calculus of bodies and spirits. Taking intensity to be the supreme value of existence is still what we all have in common. It is our condition; it is the human condition that we perhaps inherited from modernity.[6]

Intensity, whose genealogy Garcia traces to the public demonstrations of electricity in the eighteenth century, could thus be held up in opposition to the classical celebration of the golden mean. The Delphic injunction Μηδὲν ἄγαν ("Nothing in excess") stands against the currents of our age. Classicism would, then, represent the antithesis to revolution. Yet, rather than insisting on incompatibility, this book highlights a certain classicism of revolution. Its aim is to relate diverse events in the history of emancipation to a complex story of the reception of Greece and Rome. The book thus looks to the concept of revolution to understand a contested history of *classicisms*.

Indeed, the histories of "classics" as a discipline and the "age of revolutions" remain linked. Two originary moments are often isolated in the narrative of the emergence of classical scholarship: the publication of J. J. Winckelmann's *Reflections on the Imitation of Greek Masterpieces in Painting and Sculpture*, in 1755, and of Friedrich August Wolf's *Prolegomena to Homer*, in 1795. Both the literary-aesthetic yearning for Greece inaugurated by Winckelmann and the development of a rigorous philological method exemplified by Wolf took place against the background of the "age of revolutions." The invention of classical scholarship is an invention of the Enlightenment. The debates that took place about the future direction of classical studies were emerging simultaneously with the heated discussions that defined the philosophy of modernity. Immanuel Kant's short essay "What Is Enlightenment?" (1784) is its most paradigmatic statement:

> Enlightenment is man's emergence from his self-imposed immaturity. Immaturity is the inability to use one's understanding without guidance from another. This immaturity is self-imposed when its cause lies not in lack of understanding, but in lack of resolve and courage to use it without guidance from another. *Sapere Aude*! [Dare to know!] "Have courage to use your own understanding!"—that is the motto of enlightenment.[7]

One of the ironies of this famous statement is that the very motto that Kant uses to encourage us to move beyond inherited modes of thought is voiced in an inherited tongue: Latin. To live through revolution is to be trapped between the competing pulls of past and future, to experience "time out of joint."

Five years after the publication of Kant's famous essay, France would be engulfed by revolution. But it was, arguably, Kant's contemporary Moses Mendelssohn who would have a more direct effect on its unfolding. The decision to grant equal citizen rights to Jews during the French Revolution could be seen as a moment that stands at the gateway of modernity. France was the first country in Europe to emancipate the Jews in the modern age and it set a precedent for the long road to political freedom for a minority who had suffered—and had yet to suffer—centuries of oppression and persecution. The first discussion of the plight of the Jews in revolutionary France had been initiated in 1789 by the legendary Comte de Mirabeau. Speaking at a heated meeting of the revolutionary Assembly, Mirabeau proclaimed: "I haven't come to preach tolerance. Unfettered freedom of religion is to my eyes a right so sacred that the word 'tolerance' appears to me some sort of tyranny; since that implies an authority which has the right to tolerate, to weigh on the freedom of thought. We are making a Declaration of Rights," he continued: "It is absolutely necessary that [religion] be a right." He then proposed a simple formula to be included in the Declaration of the Rights of Man and of the Citizen: "No one should be troubled for his religion."[8] Mirabeau's intervention on the freedom of religion preceded a long and tortuous debate about the political rights of the Jews, and by the time emancipation was ratified by the Assembly, Mirabeau was already dead.

Rather than championing a question that was native to France, Mirabeau had instead been inspired to passionate advocacy of the Jews by a man he would call "Le Platon moderne," or the modern Plato. In the run-up to the Revolution, Mirabeau had written a biography of Mendelssohn. The Berlin philosopher was the author of another essay entitled "What Is Enlightenment?," submitted to the very same journal as Kant's more celebrated tract. He was born Moses Ben Mendel Dessau, the son of an impoverished Torah scribe. When his local rabbi moved to Berlin, the young Moses followed him and through generous patronage gained access to the intellectual and cultural elite of Prussia. Early in his career Mendelssohn set about writing a version of Plato's *Phaedo*. Appearing in 1767, Mendelssohn's own dialogue on the immortality of the soul was an immediate bestseller, published in numerous editions and widely translated in the author's lifetime.[9] His choice of dialogue is telling. The image of Socrates calmly debating his own death with his anxious followers staged a classic scene of the triumph of reason over fear and superstition. As a result, Mendelssohn would acquire the unlikely epithet of the "German Socrates."

Thus, on one reading at least, the French emancipation of the Jews owes its existence to a rereading of a Platonic dialogue. This is far from an isolated example of antiquity providing revolutionary inspiration. Twenty years after the publication of Mendelssohn's *Phaedo*, Jacques-Louis David's painting *The Death of Socrates* (figure 1) prefigured the French Revolution's call for intellectual and political liberation. Against the backdrop of the turbulent political history of the eighteenth century, Socrates had become a prominent symbol of opposition to the state. There was a proliferation of references to Socrates, as writers, artists, and philosophers all became captivated by his fate. The philosopher Denis Diderot would style his own imprisonment as a reenactment of Socrates's internment, while Edmund Burke would name Jean-Jacques Rousseau "the insane Socrates of the National Assembly."[10] Notwithstanding

FIGURE 1. Jacques-Louis David, *The Death of Socrates*, 1787. Metropolitan Museum of Art, New York, Catharine Lorillard Wolfe Collection, Wolfe Fund, 1931.

the irony of Socrates's own problematic relationship to democracy, the Athenian philosopher had become a potent symbol of intellectual and political emancipation.

David was certainly in dialogue with this wider reception of Socrates. His painting was a private commission by the aristocratic Trudaine family, who had apparently been inspired by an unfinished play about the life of Socrates by Diderot. The picture also has a particular resonance within the context of David's oeuvre. In 1775 David had traveled to Italy, where he studied both classical and Renaissance art and toured the newly excavated ruins of Pompeii. In Rome he was introduced to the German painter Anton Raphael Mengs (1728–1779). Mengs had developed a new historicizing approach to the representation of classical subjects, a precursor to the French neoclassical style we associate with David. It was also through Mengs that David was introduced to the writings of Winckelmann. *The Death of*

Socrates is the second in the sequence of David's three great classical paintings that I will discuss in this book. David's *Death of Socrates* sits midway between two powerful Roman canvasses: *The Oath of the Horatii* (1784) and *The Lictors Bring to Brutus the Bodies of His Sons* (1798). The three paintings share many formal and thematic qualities. Here we see a rigid division between the sexes, with Socrates and his male associates in the foreground, while in the background his wife, Xanthippe, is led away from the scene of his death. Plato is depicted at the end of Socrates's bed, but it is the image of Crito at Socrates's side that is perhaps more revealing. In Plato's dialogue *Crito*, it is Socrates's identity as a citizen that is at stake. There Socrates argues for the necessity of obeying the laws of the state despite the injustice of his own imprisonment and execution. His argument rests on the idea of a social contract between the citizens and the laws that govern them. David's Socrates lies on a spectrum between Plato and Rousseau. Yet, the politics of David's painting have been a source of contention. The picture was commissioned in the prerevolutionary era by the aristocrat Trudaine, who seven years later would find his way to the guillotine. It was through its print reproduction during the Revolution, rather than its original form, that *The Death of Socrates* took on its polemic force. The painting's ostensible political message shifts in tandem with the artist's ideological journey through the 1790s.[11]

But the appeal of antiquity here is only partly conveyed through the scene's ambiguous ideological content. Socrates is as much an icon of aestheticism as he is a political revolutionary. Because this Socrates isn't just intellectually powerful, he is also *beautiful*. In direct contrast to the Platonic Socrates, whose inner beauty is memorably contrasted to his outer ugliness, the attractiveness of David's Socrates could not be more manifest in its bodily form. Despite being over seventy at the time of his death, this Socrates has the body of a young Greek athlete. As Emily Wilson writes: "Far more than any of his artistic predecessors, David makes Socrates look attractive. He inspires his philosophers by his shining intelligence and his sexiness."[12] Indeed, it is Socrates's bodily frame that is literally enlightened in the picture while many of his companions are shrouded in darkness. Rather than advocating a flight from the flesh, David depicts his Socrates as a philosopher with a six-pack.

In his representation of Socrates, David betrays the influence of Winckelmann. For it is in Winckelmann's writings that the aesthetic appreciation of the Greeks goes hand in hand with a celebration of their politics. Winckelmann had famously asserted that "it was through freedom that art [among the Greeks] advanced."[13] He would later elaborate:

> The same freedom that was the mother of great occurrences, changes of regime, and emulation among the Greeks, planted as it were at the moment of its birth the seeds of a noble and sublime way of thinking; and just as the sight of the unbounded surface of the sea and the beating of the majestic waves on the cliffs of the shore expands our outlook, and makes the mind indifferent to any lowly considerations, so in the sight of such great occasions and men it was impossible to think ignobly.[14]

For Winckelmann, questions of beauty cannot be divorced from the political and moral climate that gives birth to the arts and ideals of a nation. Because Socrates was a product of Greek society and because his thought was free, he could not but be beautiful. Although Winckelmann associated the high point of Greek art with the ascendancy of Athenian democracy and was critical of the Hellenistic age and its system of royal patronage, his writings were sufficiently vague that it was possible to associate

Socrates, a fierce critic of democracy, with the ideal of freedom. In fact, it is a Winckelmannian concept of freedom that helps explain how a politically ambivalent figure like Socrates could become such a touchstone for radicalism in the eighteenth century.

More than a century later, an identification with Socrates would again prove transformative when the young Mohandas K. Gandhi crafted a Gujarati translation of Plato's *Apology* from his prison cell in South Africa. Working as a lawyer, Gandhi had increasingly become involved in civil rights activism. The Transvaal government's act compelling registration of all Indians in the colony led to mass protests and Gandhi's imprisonment. Gandhi's translation was published serially in 1908 in the newspaper *Indian Opinion*, which he founded. Entitled *Story of a Soldier of Truth*, Gandhi's reworking of Plato provided an early script for his nonviolent resistance to the colonial state. In the preface to the translation, Gandhi characterizes Socrates as a virtuous and pious individual, yet these personal qualities are linked to a wider social purpose: "A reformer, he strove to cleanse Athens, the capital of Greece [sic], of the evil which had entered its [political] life.... [Socrates's teachings] had the result of putting to an end the unconscionable gains made by persons. It came in the way of those who lived by exploiting others."[15] Socrates's critique of the money-making Sophists and the corruption of the political class is here allied to denunciation of the colonial situation in South Africa.

Yet what is most striking about Gandhi's mobilization of Socrates is the turn inward. Rather than a direct call to arms *against* the British, the text is an exhortation to a profound introspection for the Indian people:

> If, through cowardice or fear or dishonour or death, we fail to realize or recognize our shortcomings..., we shall do no

good to India's cause, notwithstanding the external remedies we may adopt, notwithstanding the Congress sessions, not even by becoming extremists. . . . When the disease is diagnosed and its true nature revealed in public, and when through suitable remedies, the body [politic] of India is cured and cleansed both within and without, it will become immune to the germs of the disease, that is to the oppression by the British and the others.[16]

Gandhi puts Socrates to a particular use in his striking biopolitical diagnosis of imperialism: "He was . . . a great Satyagrahai. He adopted Satyagraha [truth-force] against his own people."[17] Socrates is enlisted as a soldier *of truth*. A figure who speaks truth not only to the external oppressor but also to himself: "We have much to struggle for, not only in South Africa but in India as well. Only when we succeed in these [tasks] can India be rid of its many afflictions. We must learn to live and die like Socrates."[18]

Gandhi's Socratic script for civil disobedience stands in contrast to Frantz Fanon's analysis of the colonial predicament: "National liberation, national renaissance, the restoration of nationhood to a people, commonwealth: whatever may be the headings used or the new formulations introduced, decolonization is always a violent phenomenon."[19] For Fanon, the violence of colonial appropriation can be answered only by force: "Their first encounter was marked by violence and their existence together—that is to say the exploitation of the native by the settler—was carried on by dint of a great array of bayonets and cannon."[20] Nevertheless, Gandhi's reference to Socrates as a soldier is not merely figurative. He recognizes that resistance against the regime in South Africa will require bravery and courage, as later he comes to recognize that India's fight for independence may call for a kind of martyrdom. Political revolutions come in many different forms, but they are almost always accompanied by violence. The guillotine has become the symbol of the inexorable march from idealism to the reality that Fanon makes stark: "decolonization"—one could substitute "revolution"—"is quite simply the replacing of a certain 'species' of men by another 'species' of men. Without any period of transition, there is a total, complete, and absolute substitution."[21] Fanon's insistence on a lack of transition defines his revolutionary purpose against the liberal hope of reform.

Despite his very different attitude to violence, Martin Luther King Jr. shared Fanon's mistrust of patient improvement: "For years now," Dr. King states, "I have heard the word 'Wait!' It rings in the ear of every Negro with piercing familiarity. This 'Wait' has almost always meant 'Never.' We must come to see, with one of our distinguished jurists, that 'justice too long delayed is justice denied.'"[22] King was, of course, profoundly influenced by Gandhi, and like him would find a companion in Socrates, during his imprisonment in Alabama: "Just as Socrates felt that it was necessary to create a tension in the mind so that individuals could rise from the bondage of myths and half truths to the unfettered realm of creative analysis and objective appraisal, so must we see the need for nonviolent gadflies to create the kind of tension in society that will help men rise from the dark depths of prejudice and racism to the majestic heights of understanding and brotherhood."[23]

The French Revolution, in many ways, still functions as a shorthand for talking about modernity. Writing in the last century, François Furet claimed: "The Revolution does not simply 'explain' our contemporary history; it *is* our contemporary history.... For the same reason that the Ancien Régime is thought to have an end but no beginning, the Revolution has a birth and no end. For the one, seen negatively and lacking chronological definition, only its death is a certainty, for the other contains a promise of such magnitude that it becomes boundlessly elastic."[24] "The age of revolutions," in a phrase popularized by Eric Hobsbawm, was characterized by the restless pursuit of human emancipation modeled on the ideals of 1789. Is it plausible that we are still pursuing its promise?

In the more narrow sphere of political revolution, using the French Revolution as paradigm has certainly come under criticism. In *On Revolution*, Arendt anticipates Furet by exposing how the complicated superimposition of Marx and the French Revolution has shaped our contemporary conceptions. In the wake of Marx, writes Arendt, "revolutions had come under the sway of the French Revolution in general and under the predominance of the social question in particular."[25] It is in order to get beyond Marx and to reestablish the true political meaning of revolution as the search for freedom that Arendt prioritizes the American over the French Revolution in her book. Arendt and Furet both show how the narratives of revolution often involve multilayered historical perspectives. Indeed, it is perhaps because of the perceived failures of the Russian and Chinese Revolutions that European intellectuals willfully continue to foreground the French Revolution as a turning point. As Christopher Bayly and Sujit Sivasundaram, among others, have shown, the Euro-American framework obscures parallel movements of political change that took effect on a global scale during the course of the long nineteenth century and into the twentieth.[26] The French Revolution may thus be an inadequate framework for making sense of Gandhi's *Satyagraha*. Nevertheless, the example of Martin Luther King Jr. invoking Gandhi while quoting Socrates demonstrates how many political movements are a palimpsest of global currents. Reinhart Koselleck is right that "our concept of 'revolution' cannot be defined save as a flexible general concept, which may find *a priori* general consensus everywhere but whose precise meaning is subject to considerable variations from one country to another and one political field to another."²⁷

In this book I exploit the ambiguity at the heart of the term *revolution* to unravel the complex temporalities involved in modernity's yearning for the new. I will explore ancient citations in the discourse of revolutions by figures such as Mirabeau, David, and Gandhi and theorizations of revolutions by thinkers such as Karl Marx, Hannah Arendt, C. L. R. James, and Jacques Derrida, which have repeatedly foregrounded an engagement with the classical. I also analyze ancient texts to investigate antiquity's own conceptualization of continuity and rupture and antiquity's role in the foundation of political ideals. The book is structured in three chapters. The first, "Time," uses the French revolutionary calendar to reflect on how political attempts to frame history encounter the paradox of novelty. Why, when they insist on the unprecedented nature of their struggles, did the revolutionaries "anxiously conjure up the spirits of the past"?²⁸ The second chapter, "Genre," looks to the historiography of insurrection and how the classical genres of tragedy, comedy, and epic have shaped the accounts of revolutionary hope and failure. The final chapter, "Fraternity," looks at the trope of brotherhood to investigate how ancient family dynamics come to mold modern ideas of the state and its overthrow. My lens is necessarily selective, and I have decided to make the French Revolution a guiding thread. My aim, though, is not to write an intellectual history of the role of the classics in the political movements of the eighteenth century. Rather, I use the example of French revolutionaries' appeals to antiquity and the reception of those appeals in the work of a series of exemplary theorists to explore the genealogical connections between antiquity and the emancipatory movements of modernity. I also consider the French Revolution alongside a series of other rebellions, from the

Haitian slave revolt to the feminist and queer movements of the twentieth and twenty-first century. The book is not an account of revolutionary movements but of the role of the past in the narration of modern revolt.

The influence of antiquity over modernity, especially in Germany, has often been framed as a form of tyranny. Yet, the narrative I sketch is more one of tyrannicide than of tyranny. The classics have been a resource for projects of emancipation, repeatedly called on to overturn tyranny, intellectual and political. Key to Kant's vision of Enlightenment was a call to free ourselves from the strictures of the past, and yet it turns out that it was through Latin and the legacy of Greco-Roman thought that the modern world could find its liberation from received ideas. Kant, then, does not so much advocate emancipation from the past as emancipation *through* the past. This is why David saw shades of Socrates's heroism in the death of the revolutionary Jean-Paul Marat, and Mirabeau saw no contradiction in naming Moses Mendelssohn the modern Plato. The ancients have inspired a revolutionary ardor and have been caught up in both the promise and frequently the deceptions and illusions of modernity. "Resistance," as Simon Goldhill reminds us, "is also the scene of self-deception, self-interest and disavowed internal conflict."[29]

If we turn to David's depiction of Brutus in his painting *The Lictors Bring to Brutus the Bodies of His Sons* (figure 2), this intoxication with antiquity should give us pause to think. The painting was commissioned, ironically, by King Louis XVI but became a hymn to republicanism, which foretold the Revolution's own act of tyrannicide. David depicts the first Brutus, Lucius Junius Brutus, grieving for his sons. After the overthrow of Tarquinius Superbus, the last king of Rome, and the establishment of the Roman Republic, Brutus's sons attempted to restore the monarchy. Their father ordered their death and

FIGURE 2. Jacques-Louis David, *The Lictors Bring to Brutus the Bodies of His Sons*, 1789. Musée du Louvre, Paris. Digital image: incamerastock / Alamy Stock Photo.

became the heroic defender of the republic, at the expense of his own family. Can we detect in David's dark representation of a brooding Brutus a forewarning as well as a celebration? Others have read this picture as prescient of the Terror. The canvas may be asking us to look harder at where tyranny lies: Is it to be located in the treason of Brutus's sons, or is it also present in Brutus's intransigence? Is there inevitably a price to pay for the heroism of antiquity? Here is Marx writing about the effect of Rome on the French revolutionaries:

> In the classically austere traditions of the Roman Republic its gladiators found the ideals and the art forms, the self-deceptions that they needed in order to conceal from themselves the bourgeois limitations of the content of their

struggles and to keep their enthusiasm on the high plane of the great historical tragedy.[30]

For Marx, the appeal of Rome to the actors of the French Revolution was to raise their comparatively petty struggles to the "high plane of great historical tragedy." The heroism of Rome concealed the essential incompleteness of their emancipation—the failure of their revolution. For Marx it would take a new revolution—a communist revolution—to bring about real liberation.

We could perhaps see a parallel here in the false dawn of the emancipation of the Jews in 1791. The efforts of the modern Plato, Mendelssohn, would certainly not single-handedly bring about the lasting enfranchisement of the Jews. And it is difficult not to think forward from Marx to Russia and China and the communist revolutions of the twentieth century, whose aftermaths we are arguably still living through today. But Marx's reference to tragedy here gives us a different and more helpful way of thinking about the role of antiquity. Because David's picture is not all about Brutus's heroism; it is also about the tragedy of revolution depicted on the right side of the image. One's eye is as much drawn to this scene of mourning and devastation as it is to the stoic suffering of the republican hero, at left. As Marx indicates, antiquity does not just provide the vocabulary for heroic emulation; it also gives us a semantics of suffering and empathy. It is to antiquity that modernity has turned to represent the thrill of liberation *and* the pain and disappointment that can so often follow in its wake. It is to *both* its epics *and* its tragedies, its tyrannies and its tyrannicide, its world-building and its violent destruction, that the modern world continually turns to understand itself anew.

Time

If the French Revolution is the epochal marker of modernity— a "world" event in that it sets the schedule and tempo against which past and future history is henceforth measured—this is not because it provides a fixed or objective (strictly speaking, ahistorical) standard of comparison, but because it introduces untimeliness itself as an ineluctable condition of historical experience.

REBECCA COMAY

What could be more universal than time? Yet thinkers and scholars have become ever more convinced that the ancient and modern worlds are divided by their competing conceptions of chronology.[1] The story goes that the meaning of time and thus the experience of history were radically changed during the course of the eighteenth century. This rupture in the understanding of time is said to be constitutive of modernity as such. The rise of historicism, as a professionalized model for understanding the past, is just one of the more concrete manifestations of this wider transition. The French Revolution always plays an important role in this story. On the one hand, it simply acts as a marker of modernity and its new understanding of the historical. Phrases such as "since the French Revolution" have become a convenient way of speaking about the modern period. At a basic level the French Revolution coincides chronologically with the writings of figures who were crucial to defining historicism. At a more concrete level, the invention of the Republican calendar by the revolutionaries inaugurated a new model for the measurement of time that stands metonymically for its transformation. On the other hand, the concept of revolution as such helps us to get to grips with the paradoxes of time. These paradoxes find their best expression in the messy collision of ancient and modern in the French Revolution.

In this chapter I will be focusing on two paradigmatic understandings of the role of time in revolution—those formulated by the political theorists Karl Marx and Hannah Arendt. Both theorists examine how the reference to antiquity in the French Revolution complicates its claim to novelty. Both also show how the revolutionaries' sense of past injustice propels them toward an uncertain future. In discussing the concept of time, however, neither is invested in the reality of timing or duration. Rather, what interests them—and me—is the self-perception of a narrativized history. Ultimately, they reveal how the experience of revolution "introduces untimeliness itself as an ineluctable condition of historical experience."[2]

THE REPUBLICAN CALENDAR AND THE IRONIES OF TIME

In her book *On Revolution*, published in 1963, Arendt starts by asking why revolution had become one of the dominant modes of political expression in modernity:

> Wars and revolutions—as though events had only hurried up to fulfil Lenin's prediction—have thus far determined the physiognomy of the twentieth century. And as distinguished from the nineteenth-century ideologies—such as nationalism and internationalism, capitalism and imperialism, socialism and communism, which, though still invoked by

many as justifying causes, have lost contact with the major realities of our world—war and revolutions still constitute its two central political issues. They have outlived all ideological justifications. In a constellation that poses the threat of total annihilation through war against the hope for the emancipation of all mankind through revolution—leading one people after the other in quick succession "to assume among the powers of the earth the separate and equal station to which the Laws of Nature and of Nature's God entitle them"—no cause is left but the most ancient of all, the one, in fact, that from the beginning of our history has determined the very existence of politics, the cause of freedom versus tyranny.[3]

One of the most striking aspects of the opening of *On Revolution* is the complex temporalities that Arendt sets in play. While ostensibly writing about the distinctiveness of the "physiognomy of the twentieth century," Arendt brings a number of other historical horizons into view. First, the grand narratives of the nineteenth century, narratives that she had examined at length in her genealogical investigation of the origins of totalitarianism. While wars and revolutions persist, the nineteenth-century ideologies that sustained them have seemingly been left behind. Despite the apparent obsolescence of past ideological frameworks, it is Thomas Jefferson's late eighteenth-century Declaration of Independence that is invoked as the mantra of the succession of peoples' yearning for emancipation. But if the American Revolution provides the script for the revolutions of the twentieth century, it is ultimately antiquity that makes political expression possible as such: "No cause is left but the most ancient of all, the one, in fact, that from the beginning of our history has determined the very existence of politics, the cause of freedom versus tyranny." For all the distinctiveness of the twentieth-century moment, for Arendt, its events remain illegible without reference to "the most ancient of all" political framings. The tripartite temporal reference that Arendt sets up in this opening paragraph recurs as a pattern throughout *On Revolution*. Antiquity, the late eighteenth century, and the contemporary condition continuously merge in her analysis.

While Arendt's interest in revolution is motivated in part by a return to what she terms the most ancient idea of freedom, she is less convinced that revolution is itself an ancient idea. "Historically," she writes, "wars are among the oldest phenomena of the recorded past while revolutions, properly speaking, did not exist prior to the modern age; they are among the most recent of all political data."[4] Arendt establishes revolution as an inescapable "metaphor" of the modern condition:

> The modern concept of revolution, inextricably bound up with the notion that the course of history suddenly begins anew, that an entirely new story never known or told before, is about to unfold, was unknown prior to the two great revolutions at the end of the eighteenth century. Before they were engaged in what then turned out to be a revolution, none of the actors had the slightest premonition of what the plot of the new drama was going to be. However, once the revolutions had begun to run their course, and long before those who were involved in them could know whether their enterprise would end in victory or disaster, the novelty of the story and the innermost meaning of its plot became manifest to actors and spectators alike. . . . As to the plot, it was unmistakably the emergence of freedom: in 1793, four years after the outbreak of the French Revolution, at a time when Robespierre could define his rule as the "despotism of liberty" without fear of being accused of speaking in paradoxes, Condorcet summed up what everybody knew: "The word 'revolutionary' can be applied only to revolutions whose aim is freedom."[5]

The establishment of a new calendar by the French revolutionaries is a powerful metaphor for the transformation of temporality enacted by these revolutions (the Soviet calendar would later perform a similar role).[6] The Republican calendar celebrated the age of liberty in the aftermath of the proclamation of the Republic and was in use for about twelve years, from late 1793 until 1805, shortly after the coronation of Napoleon I as emperor. The calendar installed twelve thirty-day months consisting of three ten-day weeks and was part of the broader efforts of decimalization championed in the Enlightenment. The introduction of a new calendar, as it were, "begins history anew." But the rhetoric of this renewal is worth exploring in more detail. The French Republican calendar was proclaimed on September 22, 1793. This day was chosen to coincide with the autumn equinox. As Sanja Perovic writes:

> According to the gospel of the French Revolution, history began anew on the very day that a natural equality between day and night was observed. For Gilbert Romme, the calendar's chief architect, the calendar marked the epoch when the history of the French Revolution converged with nature itself, when natural equality and the power of human beings over history became one and the same. Thanks to the new calendar, the Revolution's rupture with the past was to be transformed into a wholly new experience of time, one made according to the joint dictates of nature and reason.[7]

The creation of a new calendar can be regarded as a political act of great efficacy. Time becomes the matrix through which the revolutionaries' distance from all previous cultural and religious forms can be measured. In creating a new calendar they simultaneously turn their back on classical (Roman) and Christian chronology.

Such a double rejection reminds us of the fissures *within*

ancient time. Christian time enacted a fundamental shift in the understanding of chronology in the Greco-Roman world.[8] In enacting its break with classical and religious time, the calendar cloaks itself in the rhetoric of the natural. The names of its months replace Roman emperors with names derived from the seasons (the words *Thermidor*, *Fructidor*, and so on remain all Latin and Greek, of course, and were imaged in classicizing guise). But as the quotation above makes clear, time was *naturalized* at a more profound level. The break with history is a way of resynchronizing human experience with the natural order. The calendar is what Roland Barthes would describe as an act of mythology. It represents an attempt to naturalize what is in fact deeply ideological: a political event subsumed into the rhythms of nature. In an engraving by Philibert-Louis Debucourt (figure 3), we see the allegorical figure of Philosophy inscribing the calendar into the book of Nature; the objects strewn at her feet represent the obsolescent methods of dividing time, described as "monuments of error and superstition."[9] The decision to *change* time paradoxically removes time as an explanatory factor in its creation. If secular time can be defined as the time in which humans act, this denial of human agency is made in the name of a different temporality. Human time is subordinated to cosmic time. So while, on the one hand, the invention of a new calendar performs the novelty of the revolution, on the other, by returning time to nature, it reinscribes its events in continuity.

This continuity takes several forms. The new calendar that seemingly marked a break with religion and inaugurated a new secular and rational era reinscribed the Christian premises it sought to overturn. As Charles Taylor observes, "The new French revolutionary calendar . . . draws heavily on Judaeo-Christian apocalyptic."[10] It was the Judeo-Christian conception of the apocalypse that first introduced the idea of the end

FIGURE 3. Philibert-Louis Debucourt, *Calendrier républicain*, Musée de la Révolution Française / Domaine de Vizille. Digital image: gallica.bnf.fr / BNF.

of time itself—a crucial notion for the renewal that the revolutionary calendar heralded. Moreover, the structural similarities with the Christian calendar are evident: "Just as Christianity is a religion based on the event of Christ's birth, death and Resurrection—which forever changed the meaning of history—so too the Revolution understood itself as a rupture in time that forever changed the meaning of history."[11]

It would, thus, be possible to see the calendar as a manifestation of Carl Schmitt's central insight of political theology: "All significant concepts of the modern theory of the state are secularized theological concepts not only because of their historical development—in which they were transferred from theology to the theory of the state, whereby, for example, the omnipotent God became the omnipotent lawgiver—but also because of their systematic structure, the recognition of which is necessary for a sociological consideration of these concepts."[12] This was the conclusion that Schmitt reached about modernity in his attempt to isolate the political from economic and religious spheres. The French Revolution's attempt to create a political time independent of religion simultaneously disavowed its politicality while modeling itself structurally on the religious time it sought to overturn.

Similarly, the calendar that proclaims a new form of history might instead reinstall what is in fact a very old conception. In her essay "The Concept of History," Arendt starkly differentiates the classical understanding of history from its modern successor:

> In order to understand quickly and with some measure of clarity how far we today are removed from [the] Greek understanding of the relationship between nature and history, between the cosmos and men, we may be permitted to quote four lines from Rilke . . . ["Mountains rest beneath a splendor of stars, but even in them time flickers. Ah, unsheltered in my wild, darkling heart lies immortality."] Here even the mountains only seem to rest under the light of the stars; they are slowly, secretly devoured by time; nothing is forever, immortality has fled the world to find an uncertain abode in the darkness of the human heart that still has the capacity to remember and to say: forever. Immortality or imperishability, if and when it occurs at all, is homeless.[13]

For Arendt, it is the relationship between nature and history that fundamentally divides the ancient from the modern experience. It was against the backdrop of imperishable nature that the Greeks reflected on the tragedy of human finitude. History, for them, was a way to counteract the inescapable futility of human action, which in contrast to the cosmos was all too perishable. So Arendt continues:

> If one looks upon these lines through Greek eyes it is almost as though the poet had tried consciously to reverse the Greek relationships: everything has become perishable, except perhaps the human heart; immortality is no longer the medium in which mortals move, but has taken its homeless refuge in the very heart of mortality; immortal things, works and deeds, events and even words, though men might still be able to externalize, reify as it were, the remembrance of their hearts, have lost their home in the world; since the world, since nature is perishable and since man-made things, once they come into being, share the fate of all being—they begin to perish the moment they have come into existence.[14]

The permanence of nature that the Greeks took for granted is no longer a given of modernity. Cosmic time becomes subject to the same vicissitudes as human history.

Arendt's account of ancient and modern here builds on the traditional opposition between cyclical and linear time. While the Greeks and Romans are said to have operated with a cyclical notion, Christianity and then modernity in its wake replaced this circular conception with a directional one. In this famous passage from the *City of God*, Augustine highlights how Christian time marks a decisive break with cyclicality:

> Our present concern is to refute that cyclic theory according to which the same things must always be repeated at peri-

odic intervals. Yet no matter which of the interpretations mentioned of "ages of ages" is correct, it has no bearing on these cycles. For whether the term "ages of ages" means, not a repetition of the same ages, but a succession of different ages, running on one after the other, with perfectly ordered connexion, while the bliss of delivered souls remains most secure without any return of miseries, or whether the "ages of ages" are eternal, standing in relation to those of time as master to subject, there is no place for those cyclic repetitions, which are utterly refuted by the eternal life of the saints.[15]

But the conventional opposition grounded in passages such as Augustine's has come under pressure for many years from classicists such as Arnaldo Momigliano, who rightly regard it as too simplistic.[16] To quote Astrid Möller and Nino Luraghi: "We cannot label one culture cyclical and another linear, because most people perceive time in different ways, according to their contexts and situations, with the result that any one culture is characterized" by a variety of approaches to time.[17] Nevertheless, from Heraclitus to Augustine, it is clear that the circle and the cycle operated as powerful metaphors for time, and that these metaphors had a profound impact on ancient thematizations of agency.

For Arendt, Herodotus exemplifies the Greek perspective: while he celebrated individual extraordinary actions in the hope of saving them from obscurity, he did so without subordinating them to a grander idea of History. What distinguishes modernity is the belief in the possibility of men "making" History. This is what is at stake in the revolutionaries' unshakable belief in the novelty of their experience. And yet, in the creation of the revolutionary calendar, they appear to make history and at the same time disavow their agency. By cloaking the calendar in the language of nature, they invoke cosmic cyclicality and downplay human action. Perovic outlines the paradoxes of the calendar:

> The Republican calendar was crucial in combining two aspects of revolutionary time that proved, in the end, to be at odds: the belief in history as linear progress and the desire for a collective moral and political regeneration that can only take place in cyclical time.... How did a Revolution that first staged itself as regeneration, that is, as restoration, of a better past, come to think of itself under the symbol of rupture? In other words, how did a Revolution that turned to a new calendar in order to regenerate history into the natural and cyclical time of planetary "revolutions" come to define itself as an irreversible and linear change?[18]

It is precisely this tension between the wholly new and the regeneration of a "better past" that the calendar performs. For it is not only in its invocation of cyclical time that the calendar displays its debt to a specifically *classical* past. From its Greco-Latinate names to its neoclassical imagery (see figure 4, where the month Frimaire appears in the guise of the Greek/Roman goddess Artemis/Diana), the calendar mirrors the Revolution more broadly by clothing itself in ancient garb. For the critic Rebecca Comay, the calendar enacts the anachronism at the heart of revolution itself. She writes: "The new republican calendar that was introduced belatedly, in the Year II, by order of the Convention (after weeks and months of vacillation about when the new era had actually started, what was to mark the beginning, what would establish the terms of measurement, and what exactly was to be commemorated), the Revolution immediately became obsolete.... It is anachronism that produces both the singularity of revolution and its terrible

FIGURE 4. *Frimaire* (November/December), third month of the Republican calendar, engraved by Salvatore Tresca, ca. 1794, after Louis Lafitte (1770–1828). Musée de la Ville de Paris. Digital image: CC0 Paris Musées / Musée Carnavalet—Histoire de Paris.

insufficiency—both its irrepressible novelty and its insufferable need for repetition."[19] For Comay, to live revolution is to experience "time out of joint." Constantly buffered between past and future—the failure of the past and the (never realized) hope of the future—the present becomes fissured.

IMITATION AND INNOVATION

The French Revolution, Arendt tells us, created the possibility of composing a "new story." It was the revolutionaries' perception of the novelty of their aspirations that was so key to their motivation. Their new story would deviate from all preexisting emplotments. But despite the potential afforded by this new narrative freedom, Arendt encodes the revolutionaries' actions within a particular generic framework. As the revolutionaries in her text assume the role of actors, their revolution becomes a drama. The theater of revolution transforms citizens into actors and witnesses into spectators.[20] Arendt's turn of phrase in this passage is far from casual. In imagining the French Revolution as a drama, Arendt invokes Greek tragedy and its distinctive exploration of freedom and human agency.[21] The philosophy of the tragic formulated in German idealist philosophy, which emerged in the French Revolution's wake, not only seeks to thematize the perpetuity of the conflict between freedom and necessity; it also casts us all as actors in and spectators of the drama that ensues. Before she even invokes Robespierre's "despotism of liberty," her own narrative is framed by the poles of freedom and necessity. The same paradoxical relationship between freedom and necessity, despotism and liberty, that forms the basis of idealism's analysis of tragedy seems to pervade Arendt's description of the theater of revolution. The plot that characterizes revolution is the same plot that structures tragedy. Robespierre's "despotism of liberty" reenacts the classic formulation of Oedipus's tragic dilemma, as formulated in Friedrich Schelling's reading of Sophocles's play. Oedipus, as Schelling demonstrated, was himself subject to a dictatorship of freedom: despite the fact that his actions were the product of necessity he took responsibility for them as if they were an expression of his freedom—and it is this self-conviction that amounts to his freedom (in self-destruction). We will see in the following chapter how Arendt's metaphor recalls contemporary and later accounts of the French Revolution in dramatic terms. It also deepens her own analysis of the key role that freedom plays in the modern experience and theorization of revolution.

Arendt considers the American and French Revolutions to be distinctive in that they *combine* the pursuit of freedom with striving after the wholly new. As Arendt phrases it: "Crucial to any understanding of revolutions in the modern age is that the idea of freedom and the experience of a new beginning should coincide."[22] In this combination of freedom and novelty Arendt constructs a complicated ancient genealogy for revolution. For the sense of beginning that Arendt associates with the eighteenth-century revolutionaries does not just run in parallel; it is itself structurally related to the idea of freedom. And this idea of freedom, far from being something wholly new, was in part nothing more than the recovery of an ancient idea:

> What the revolutions brought to the fore was this experience of being free, and this was a new experience, not, to be sure, in the history of Western mankind—it was common enough in both Greek and Roman antiquity—but with regard to the centuries which separate the downfall of the Roman Empire from the rise of the modern age. And this relatively new experience, new to those at any rate who made it, was at the same time the experience of man's faculty to begin some-

thing new. These two things together—a new experience which revealed man's capacity for novelty—are at the root of the enormous pathos we find in both the American and French Revolutions, this ever repeated instance that nothing comparable in grandeur and significance had ever happened in the whole recorded history of mankind, and which, if we had to account for it in terms of successful reclamation of civil rights, would sound entirely out of place.

Only where this pathos of novelty is present and where novelty is connected with the idea of freedom are we entitled to speak of revolution.[23]

What is crucial to the eighteenth-century revolutionaries is that they experienced freedom as something wholly new, as something unprecedented in human history. The idea of freedom that they attempted to enshrine in their actions and institutions could not be understood as a mere extension of "civil rights" that previous political movements had vindicated.

And yet, as Arendt points out, the experience of freedom they advocated "was common enough in both Greek and Roman antiquity":

> Modern revolutions have little in common with the mutatio rerum of Roman history or the stasis, the civil strife which disturbed the Greek polis. We cannot equate them with Plato's μεταβολαί [*metabolai*,] the quasi-natural transformation of one form of government into another, or with Polybius's πολιτειῶν ἀνακύκλωσις [*politeion anakuklosis*], the appointed recurring cycle into which human affairs are bound by reason of their always being driven to extremes. Antiquity was well acquainted with political change and the violence that went with change, but neither of them appeared to it to bring about something altogether new. Changes did

not interrupt the course of what the modern age has called history, which, far from starting with a new beginning, was seen as falling back into a different stage of the cycle, prescribing a course which was preordained by the very nature of human affairs and which therefore was unchangeable.[24]

In book 8 of the *Republic*, for instance, Plato gives a dramatic account of the succession of political constitutions from aristocracy through timocracy, oligarchy through democracy and finally to tyranny. In these passages, Plato describes political change as the result of an overreach within a particular political system that almost inevitably precipitates a transition to a preexisting alternative order. Notwithstanding the utopian dimension of the *Republic* itself, Plato's schema in book 8 does not imagine the coming into existence of a wholly new order:

> A city which is thus constituted can hardly be shaken; but, seeing that everything which has a beginning has also an end, even a constitution such as yours will not last for ever, but will in time be dissolved. And this is the dissolution:—In plants that grow in the earth, as well as in animals that move on the earth's surface, fertility and sterility of soul and body occur when the circumferences of the circles of each are completed, which in short-lived existences pass over a short space, and in long-lived ones over a long space.[25]

With its language of cycles and metaphors of the natural, Plato's account of political change here seems decidedly premodern. There is no sense of men making their own history. It seems difficult to reconcile this account, grounded in the circle of nature, with Plato's revolutionary depiction of *Kallipolis* itself. Polybius's later analysis of the cycle of regimes, which would be extremely influential over a long period of time, shares Plato's emphasis on nature. For Polybius, *anakuklosis* refers to the succession of constitutions in a continuous, law-abiding cycle, *kata phusin*, according to nature (6.5.1). Plato and Polybius exemplify a pre-eighteenth-century understanding that stayed close to the etymological roots of the word *revolution*, seeing political change as cyclical development rather than as inaugurating a previously unimagined social organization.

Arendt picks up the Greek semantics.[26] In Greek, there are three terms that seem particularly relevant: *stasis*, which names a conflict and is always troped negatively, *neoterizein* which connotes disruption and desire for change and is likely to lead to *stasis*; and finally *metabole* (pl. *metabolai*), the term used by Plato to denote a change of power. It is a neutral, analytic term to describe shifts in power: oligarchy becomes democracy becomes oligarchy; big cities become small, small cities big. Aristotle would use this same word in his description of the causes of violent political change in book 5 of the *Politics*. But for Aristotle, *metabole* does not necessarily imply the overthrow of a particular constitution; for example, he speaks of the intensification of oligarchic tendencies within an existing oligarchic system. Although Aristotle's account is largely analytical, it is clear that his concern is to moderate the scope and pace of change. It is precisely the safeguards against such changes that seem to motivate his discussion. As Arendt argues, none of these terms or their discussion by ancient political theorists gets close to what modernity invests in revolution. Revolution requires not just a change in who has power, nor just a systemic change (this is a necessary if not sufficient condition), but also a change in how an individual relates to power structures. Thus in both the French and American Revolutions a subject of the crown becomes the citizen of a republic—and this is fundamental. Moreover, for Arendt, the notion of "beginning"—which is rectilinear and belongs therefore to a modern temporality—is particular to modern revolutions, and her definition of revolution makes it synonymous with this exclusively modern phenomenon or experience of the new.

Arendt's equivocation over the novelty of the revolutionary can, of course, be mapped onto a wider debate about the term *revolution* and the influence of ancient debates about political change.[27] As Koselleck writes: "In the horizon of our experience of time in a technological-industrial age, it is easy to overlook how strong the metaphorics of return really were in the French concept of revolution."[28] The history of the term *revolution* across European languages is complex. The word only gradually came to take on political connotations and only later still would it be associated with convulsive—and irreversible—political change. For Koselleck among others, it is the French Revolution that fundamentally changed its meaning. After 1789, he writes, "Revolution obviously no longer returned to given conditions or possibilities, but has ... led forward to an unknown future."[29] And yet, as Koselleck shows, for a figure like Karl Marx, writing fifty years after the events of 1789, the term *revolution* is still not without ambiguity. For, as Koselleck shows, Marx repeatedly "resorted to the older sense of revolution as repetition, for he could not completely escape its distant echoes."[30] In *The Eighteenth Brumaire of Louis Bonaparte*, for instance, in a passage we will return to in the next chapter, Marx formulates the role of Rome in the French Revolution as an instance of history repeating itself:

> Hegel remarks somewhere that all facts and personages of great importance in world history occur, as it were, twice. He forgot to add: the first time as tragedy, the second time as farce. Caussidière for Danton, Louis Blanc for Robespierre, the *Montagne* of 1848 to 1851 for the *Montagne* of 1793 to 1795, the Nephew for the Uncle. And the same caricature

occurs in the circumstances attending the second edition of the eighteenth Brumaire!

Men make their own history, but they do not make it just as they please; they do not make it under circumstances chosen by themselves, but under circumstances directly encountered, given and transmitted from the past. The tradition of all the dead generations weighs like a nightmare on the brain of the living. And just when they seem engaged in revolutionising themselves and things, in creating something that has never yet existed, precisely in such periods of revolutionary crisis they anxiously conjure up the spirits of the past to their service and borrow from them names, battle cries and costumes in order to present the new scene of world history in this time-honoured disguise and this borrowed language.[31]

Marx here exemplifies Arendt's vision of modernity with his conviction that men *make* history. But, contra Arendt, Marx presents the idea of an unprecedented revolution as an illusion. On the one hand, Marx seems to be claiming that the French Revolution gains its meaning not despite but because of the fact that it had a precedent. On the other hand, it could be argued that Marx is proclaiming that the very innovation of the event is predicated on the return of some "spirit of the past." The "newness" of the French Revolution consists in its untimely reenactment of the "very ancient" in the "very modern."[32] "The heroes as well as the parties and the masses of the old French Revolution," Marx writes, "performed the task of their time in Roman costumes and with Roman phrases."[33] The active agents of the French Revolution achieve the "task of their time." "Men," as Marx says, "make their *own* history." This is no regressive, nostalgic backward gaze, but rather a progressive and active mobilization of the past in the present.

Walter Benjamin would later elect this moment as the

archetypal instance of what he called the *Jetztzeit*: "History is the subject of a structure whose site is not homogeneous, empty time, but time filled by the presence of the now. Thus, to Robespierre ancient Rome was a past charged with the time of the now which he blasted out of the continuum of history. The French Revolution viewed itself as Rome reincarnate."[34] In his analysis of revolution, Marx reveals how the imagery and symbols of the past act as both a spur and a restraint for the revolutionary actors in the present:

> The new social formation once established, the antediluvian Colossi disappeared and with them resurrected Romanity— the Brutuses, Gracchi, Publicolas, the tribunes, the senators, and Caesar himself. . . . Wholly absorbed in the production of wealth and in peaceful competitive struggle, it no longer comprehended that the ghosts from the days of Rome had watched over its cradle.[35]

As Derrida phrases it, "One has to forget the specter and the parody, Marx seems to say, so that history can continue. But if one is content to forget it, then the result is bourgeois platitude: life, that's all. So one must not forget it, one must remember it but while forgetting it enough, in this very memory, in order to 'find again the *spirit* of the revolution without making its *specter* return.'"[36] What is interesting is the agency that Marx ascribes to the Roman precedent. Rome is responsible at the same time for the inevitable slide into bourgeois self-satisfaction and for presenting itself as its antidote. He simultaneously reinscribes Rome in an inexorable history of bourgeois ascendancy and argues that it is precisely by *forgetting* Rome that the French have precipitated this impasse. For Marx, Rome is both the promise of an ideal and ultimately a "self-deception." But the responsibility for this self-deception rests ultimately with its receivers. Marx leaves open the possibility that Rome could be an ideal that, precisely, prevents a return to the same. In fact, if anything could save the revolutionaries from this false consciousness, it is the specter of Rome "watch[ing] over [their] cradle."

Marx's sense of historicity here is further complicated by the double referent for *the* French Revolution. For Marx's *Eighteenth Brumaire of Louis Bonaparte*, in fact, refers to at least three events in recent French history: the revolutions of 1789 and 1848 and the coup of 1851 that reversed the latter. Indeed, at stake in his discussion of *Romanitas* is an opposition between the "authentic" appropriation by the heroes of 1789 and the affectated Roman aspirations of the new Napoleon. Two revolutions, two Napoleons, two Romes: the time of revolution, as Marx reminds us, cannot help but be redoubled.

In *On Revolution*, Arendt also highlights the attachment to Roman concepts in the French Revolution and she similarly associates it with its failures. She writes of the "French *hommes de lettres* who were to make the revolution":

> They had no experience to fall back upon, only ideas and principles untested by reality to guide and inspire them. . . . Hence they depended even more on memories from antiquity, and they filled the ancient Roman words with suggestions that arose from language and literature rather than from experience. . . . However strongly the emotions of Robespierre and his colleagues may have been swayed by experiences for which there were hardly any ancient precedents, their conscious thoughts and words stubbornly return to Roman language. If we wish to draw the line in purely linguistic terms, we might insist on the relatively late date of the word "democracy," which stresses the people's rule and role, as opposed to the word "republic," with its strong emphasis

FIGURE 5. Jacques-Louis David, *The Tennis Court Oath*, 1790–94. Musée Carnavalet, Paris. Digital image: CC0 Paris Musées / Musée Carnavalet—Histoire de Paris.

on objective institutions. And the word "democracy" was not used in France until 1794; even the execution of the king was still accompanied by the shouts: *Vive la république*.[37]

Arendt, like Marx, sees the French revolutionaries' reluctance to create their own revolutionary language as a symptom of their inability to fully "make their own history." We can think here of Jacques-Louis David's Roman pictures as the ultimate figuration of this tendency. David's unfinished painting *The Tennis Court Oath* (figure 5) was intended to commemorate the symbolic origin of the Revolution, when the Third Estate, barred from entering the palace, came together as the National Assembly and swore a solemn oath to stay together until they had established a constitution.[38] The painting, which foregrounds a performance of allegiance, however, repurposes the visual vocabulary of his first great Roman painting, *The Oath of the Horatii* (figure 7, discussed in chapter 3). In a similar manner, as we have seen, the execution of the French king in 1791 is foretold by David in the depiction of Brutus's tyrannicide in his 1789 painting *The Lictors Bring to Brutus the Bodies of His Sons* (figure 2), which celebrates the establishment of the first Roman Republic.

For both Marx and Arendt, David's depictions of the Revolution are symptomatic of the revolutionaries' inability to move beyond a "borrowed language."[39] But for Arendt, it is the revolutionaries' incapacity to move beyond the Roman political vocabulary of republicanism, toward the Greek language of freedom and democracy, that ultimately holds them back. Arendt and Marx, then, share an ambivalence about the role of antiquity in providing a model for the revolutionaries of the eighteenth century. But where Marx's equivocation highlights the incompleteness of the model of emancipation inherited from the ancients, Arendt remains committed to an ancient model of freedom. In fact, Arendt believes it is only by returning to an ancient idea of freedom that revolution can emerge as a successful political force in modernity. Nevertheless, while she remains committed to that ancient model she does not advocate its restoration. She calls for a conceptual return, not one to be performed in practice. For Marx, by contrast, antiquity remains an inadequate paradigm, because the economic conditions of modernity require a completely new model of political action:

> The social revolution of the nineteenth century cannot draw its poetry from the past, but only from the future. It cannot begin with itself before it has stripped off all superstition in regard to the past. Earlier revolutions required recollections of past world history in order to drug themselves concerning their own content. In order to arrive at its own content, the revolution of the nineteenth century must let the dead bury

their dead. There the phrase went beyond the content; here the content goes beyond the phrase.[40]

Marx's *social* revolution demands a new blueprint: it needs to treat the past as dead in order to be able move beyond it. For all the power of its poetry, antiquity remains nothing more than that, an ideological self-deception that prevents modern actors from confronting the reality of their material conditions. Arendt's *political* revolution, by contrast, mandates a return to ancient notions of freedom to emancipate its actors from the modern tyranny of the social. Nevertheless, as we have seen, Arendt denies revolution to the ancients. While their understanding of freedom remains unsurpassed, it is their capacity for "beginning" that she faults:

> Only where change occurs in the sense of new beginning, where violence is used to constitute an altogether different form of government, to bring about the formation of a new body politic, where the liberation from oppression aims at least at the constitution of freedom can we speak of revolution. And the fact is that although history has known those who, like Alcibiades, wanted power for themselves or those who, like Catiline, were *rerum novarum cupidi*, eager for new things, the revolutionary spirit of the last centuries, that is the eagerness to liberate *and* to build a new house where freedom can dwell, is unprecedented and unequalled in all prior history.[41]

What is specific to modern revolution, then, is the two steps: violence against an old order and commitment to house freedom in a new one.

The question of the novelty of revolution, for Arendt as for Marx, is not one of academic historicism. The question of *his-*

tory had itself become deeply political during the course of the French Revolution. As François Hartog demonstrates, two competing understandings of the past dominated debates among the revolutionaries themselves. Marx was just one in a long line of critics who mocked the Jacobins for their purposeful imitation of the ancients—indeed, the very question of political action had become embroiled in a debate about the "imitation" of the ancients. The young François-René de Chateaubriand, writing from exile in London in 1797, would observe: "Our Revolution was brought about in part by men of letters who, more citizens of Rome and Athens than their own country, tried to bring ancient customs back to Europe."[42] The Revolution, he would later say, was "a chaos, where Jacobins met Spartans, and the *Marseillaise* melded with the songs of Tyrtaeus."[43] Already in 1795, the Comte de Volney would denounce the education system that produced this confusion:

> It is these much-vaunted classical books, these poets and orators, and these historians that, given freely without discernment to the young, imbued them with their principles or their feelings. It is these that, by offering them models of certain men and certain actions, enflamed in them a natural desire for imitation; it is these that had accustomed them under the yoke of education to become passionate for virtue and for real and imagined beauty, but since they were beyond their comprehension, in the end they only served to encourage the blind sentiment we might call "enthusiasm."[44]

In the hands of the young, the ancient world could become a dangerous illusion. Adversaries to the Jacobins thus began to formulate a script for modernity that condemned the ancients to oblivion. This countercurrent not only saw the New World as a more relevant stage for the rehearsal of political progress; it also questioned the validity of the very concept of "analogy" as a tool of historical inquiry. The Jacobins were not only politically but also historically naive. Anachronism became the bête noire of a new current of historicism. These parallel developments within the fields of political thought and historiography fused into a single discourse that saw a break with the ancient world as central to the progress of modernity. The new science of historical positivism and the proponents of representative democracy could share a single slogan: "The man of rights cannot be the citizen of an ancient Republic."[45]

This account, however, fails to do justice to the complexity of the Jacobins' stake in imitation. Enacting David's famous painting, Louis Antoine de Saint-Just had donned the mantle of Brutus in his denunciation of Louis XVI. Recall here also the doubleness of Brutus in antiquity—already a figure of emulation, already a figure who would repeat history: the first tyrant slayer standing behind the second. And yet, Saint-Just was ambivalent about the desirability and even possibility of impersonation:

> Do not doubt it, everything that exists around us is unjust; victory and liberty will cover the world. Don't despise anything, but don't imitate anything that has happened in the past before you; heroism does not have any models. This is how, I repeat, you will found a powerful empire, with the audacity of genius and the strength of justice and truth.[46]

The past should not be despised, but nor could it become a blueprint for the future. Heroism, precisely, has *no* models. Saint-Just's equivocation over imitation recalls Winckelmann's famous musings about the perfectibility of antiquity: "The only way we can become great, and, if this is possible, inimitable, is by imitating the Ancients."[47] As Alex Potts and Hartog have argued, Winckelmann had prepared the ground for the French

Revolution—it is his theories about antiquity that make David's imagery legible.[48] Winckelmann made the imitation of the Greeks a key aspiration of modernity. And yet, in its paradoxical phrasing, Winckelmann's proclamation also intimates the necessary frustrations involved in such an enterprise. So David Ferris writes: "Winckelmann, in stating that modernity must imitate if it is to become great, establishes Greece as the future possibility of history. But, what this modernity strives for in the name of Greece is less a return to antiquity than the inimitability through which the relation of antiquity to the modern is defined as a gap that may never be bridged. Modernity, in effect, seeks to affirm the necessity of its existence, and this necessity is discovered in the impossible example of Greece."[49]

Imitation and innovation, return and rupture: none of these figures fully capture the complex temporalities of revolution. Reading Saint-Just together with Winckelmann may help us make sense of David's visual artillery. Reflecting on his earlier Roman painting, David would say: "Perhaps I've revealed too much of the anatomical in my painting of the Horatii; in this one of the *Sabines*, I'll hide it with more skill and taste. This painting will be more Greek."[50] David's *Intervention of the Sabine Women* (figure 6) appears to depict the Bastille as a symbolic representation of the 1789 Revolution looming in the background of this famous scene from early Rome and its fight to overcome the Sabines. Hersilia, the Sabine wife of Romulus, throws herself between the armies and makes an entreaty for peace. Created between 1795 and 1799, the painting has been interpreted as a plea for national reconciliation in the wake of the Terror. But what does it mean for David to call his Roman painting Greek? When David reaches for more skill, more taste, he reaches past Rome to Greece. But what is it that David is attempting to *hide* in the name of Greece? The reference to antiquity becomes a kind of ever more sophisticated subter-

FIGURE 6. Jacques-Louis David, *The Intervention of the Sabine Women*, 1795–99. Musée du Louvre, Paris. Digital image: Sailko / Wikimedia (CC BY-SA 3.0, https://creativecommons.org/licenses/by-sa/3.0/deed.en).

fuge. Like the naturalizing gesture of the revolutionary calendar, the reference to antiquity is forever trying to make itself more tasteful, more skillful, and more inevitable. It is a fully conscious political gesture masking itself as a natural one.

Writing about the power of the concept of revolution as such, the French historian and philosopher Mona Ozouf shows how the paradoxes of temporality can obscure more profound questions about political agency:

> The strength of the concept of revolution comes not only from its supposedly universal validity but also, in an ambiguous way, from its ability to combine two conflicting ideas. The first, borrowed from the eighteenth-century account and also a common theme of traditionalist thought, is that

the revolution is an irresistible necessity, which enables revolutionaries to justify the heroic sacrifice of individuals to the great event and to absolve in advance any crimes that may be committed. This idea is wedded, without any genuine exploration of the problems involved, to the idea that men have absolute power over their destinies. A major symbol of historicism yet at the same time an object of individual activism, an absolutely human event, that nevertheless completely transcends individual human beings, the Revolution draws from these contradictory representations its extraordinary power of fascination.[51]

Ozouf's language here recalls Arendt and her essay "The Concept of History." There, as we saw, Arendt was keen to differentiate the modern sense of a *purposeful* history from an ancient notion of cosmic predictability. For Ozouf, the French Revolution combines this sense of transcendent inevitability with a lionization of individual political action. In this gesture, it marries cyclicality to linearity, circle to arrow, nature to history. For Ozouf, this dialectic is poorly worked through. But what I have been arguing is that it is in the reference to antiquity that such questions of agency have their fullest exploration. The French Revolution allows us to see how modernity takes its form in a failed act of rupture with the past. "Men," as Marx says, "make their history, but they do not make it just as they please; they do not make it under circumstances chosen by themselves but under circumstances directly encountered, given and transmitted from the past."[52]

Genre

"THE REVOLUTION WILL NOT BE TELEVISED"

As happened finally in all the enlightenment of modern times with the French Revolution (that terrible farce, quite superfluous when judged close at hand, into which, however, the noble and visionary spectators of all Europe have interpreted from a distance their own indignation and enthusiasm so long and passionately, until the text has disappeared under the interpretation).

FRIEDRICH NIETZSCHE, *BEYOND GOOD AND EVIL*

Chinese premier Zhou Enlai famously declared it "too soon to tell" the significance of the French Revolution of 1789. This popular anecdote brings together the concerns of my first two chapters here. The last chapter discussed the complex temporalities of revolution and the role of ancient time in their narrativization. It highlighted how the appeal to classical examples complicated the claim to innovation at the heart of modern revolutionary language. The "borrowed language" from antiquity created a loop in the progression of linear time and unspooled the revolving chronologies of revolution. This chapter looks at the related question of genre and the important role it plays in giving shape and significance to revolutionary action. Just as the meaning of revolution is often understood only in its aftereffects, the mode of narration importantly affects the experience of revolution as success or failure. In his book *Metahistory*, Hayden

White argued that history, far from consisting of a series of preexisting events that are later shaped into a story, actually exists in its retelling. The narrative form of history is integral to the experience of history—in other words, one might argue, there is no distinction between history and *metahistory*. The poetic emplotment of history as romance, tragedy, comedy, or satire is part of its essence. This chapter looks at the specific appeal of classical genres, particularly the dramatic genres of tragedy and comedy, in key accounts of the French and Haitian Revolutions.

Long before White, commentators on the French Revolution of 1789 understood its metahistorical dimension. Its aftermath produced such powerful narrativizations that they threatened to eclipse the "original" happening. This was nowhere more the case than in the German-speaking world. "German writers at the end of the eighteenth century described the French Revolution as a drama for which their front-row seats rendered them ideal spectators," writes Rebecca Comay.[1] In particular, Comay sees the French Revolution as the spectacle that enables Immanuel Kant to transform the discourse of morality into an aesthetic register. Comay continues: "In his third *Critique* (1790), [Kant] had already formalized the logic whereby terror experienced at a slight distance yields the sublime satisfaction of moral self-enhancement."[2] The imperative of disinterestedness that Kant assigns to the aesthetic sphere is transferred to the act of political spectatorship. "The logic is ultimately Aristotelian: terror is purged through a vicarious catharsis secured by aesthetic distance."[3]

And yet, in describing the reaction to the revolution in *The Conflict of the Faculties*, Kant describes not so much a catharsis as its opposite:

> The revolution of gifted people which we have seen unfolding in our day may succeed or miscarry. It may be filled with

> misery and atrocities to the point that a sensible man, were he boldly to hope to execute it successfully the second time, would never resolve to execute it at such a cost—this revolution, I say, nonetheless finds in the hearts of all spectators (who are not engaged in this game themselves) a wishful participation that borders closely on enthusiasm, the very expression of which is fraught with danger; this sympathy, therefore, can have no other cause than a moral predisposition in the human race.[4]

The reaction of horror that Kant describes encapsulates both the fascination and the fervent disappointment experienced by the onlooker. But the pity and fear evoked by the performance does not act apotropaically on the audience, but rather enjoins the bystanders to join in. This is a spectacle that breaks down the fourth wall.

For as Nietzsche makes clear, it is far from passive. The act of looking is accompanied by the work of interpretation. To Nietzsche's mind, the strength of the German interpretation is such that it overpowers the French "text" of Revolution. So while France experienced the political revolution, Germany underwent a revolution in thought. The combined forces of Kantian philosophy and later German Idealism represented an intellectual upheaval that paralleled the political turbulence in France. Heinrich Heine would later worry that "only our most distant descendants will be able to decide whether we should be praised or reproached for first working out our philosophy before working out our revolution."[5] But other writers did not so much see a parallelism as a hierarchy:

> The French Revolution, Fichte's *Wissenschaftslehre*, and Goethe's [*Wilhelm*] *Meister* are the greatest tendencies of the age. Whoever is offended by this juxtaposition, whoever

takes seriously only a revolution that is noisy and materialistic, has still not elevated himself to the broader, higher perspective on the history of mankind. Even in our shabby cultural histories, which usually resemble a collection of variants with running commentary for a lost classical text, many a little book has played a larger role than anything done by the noisy multitude, who took no notice of it at the time.[6]

Friedrich Schlegel starts off by analogizing the different "tendencies of the age," seeing Fichte's and Goethe's writings as the textual equivalents of political realities. But when he reflects self-consciously on the analogy he introduces a distinction between mere political "noise" and the "higher perspective" of philosophy. Only a person who has not "elevated himself" to the insights of German thought would confuse the "materialistic" aims of the French revolutionaries with the world-historical significance of German Romanticism. Moreover, Schlegel's text effects "a reversal of chronological and phenomenological sequence that challenges the ontological priority of the origin as such."[7] The juxtaposition obscures temporal sequence and denies the French Revolution's role as the determinative stimulus for the development of German Romanticism. But Schlegel's account also anticipates Nietzsche's later textualization of the political event. More specifically, Schlegel philologizes it. He compares the French Revolution to a "lost classical text" that has long since been eclipsed by the scholarly work of reconstruction. The long history of establishing textual variants and producing commentaries comes to overshadow the absent original.[8] Just as a Homer or a Sophocles only really comes into existence as the product of their scholarly afterlife, so the French Revolution, for Schlegel, is birthed by the reaction it provokes in German intellectual life.

For Heine and others, Schlegel's commentary represents

a defense mechanism, a psychological reaction to the realization of Germany's political backwardness. Karl Marx gave a name to this defensiveness: *Die deutsche Misère*. "We are the *philosophical* contemporaries of the modern age," writes Marx, "without being the *historical* contemporaries."[9] In *A Contribution to the Critique of Hegel's "Philosophy of Right,"* he elaborates: "The struggle against the German political present is the struggle against the past of modern nations, which continue to be harassed by the reminiscences of this past. It is instructive for them to see the *ancien régime*, which in their countries has experienced its *tragedy*, play its *comic* role, as a German phantom."[10] In bringing together my book's twined themes of fissured temporality and genre, Marx is here drawing on Hegel's aesthetics and the historical sequence Hegel charts in the evolution of literary history. Just as tragedy, in Hegel's scheme, represents a stage in the generic evolution toward comedy, the French Revolution is the tragic precursor to Germany's current farce:

> The modern *ancien régime* is merely the *clown* of a world order whose *real heroes* are dead. History is thorough and passes through many stages while bearing an ancient form to its grave. The last stage of a world-historical form is its *comedy*. The Greek gods, who already died once of their wounds in Aeschylus's tragedy *Prometheus Bound*, were forced to die a second death—this time a comic one—in Lucian's dialogues. Why does history take this course? So that mankind may part happily with its past. We lay claim to this *happy* historical destiny for the powers of Germany.[11]

Marx figures the German ancien régime of the 1840s as the parodic repetition of the rule of Louis XVI. The old order's original tragic end took place in France and must now take place in comic form in Germany. First time as Aeschylus, second time as

Lucian... While Nietzsche interprets the French Revolution as a farce that only his German *Birth of Tragedy* can remedy, Marx sees German intellectual life as the farce that encapsulates its defensive reaction to the real tragedy of France.

This is the first place in Marx's work where he employs the combined tropes of history repeating itself and the language of ancient genres. His much more famous usage of it comes a decade later, at the opening of his analysis of a *different* French Revolution, in *The Eighteenth Brumaire of Louis Bonaparte*: "Hegel remarks somewhere that all facts and personages of great importance in world history occur, as it were, twice. He forgot to add: the first time as tragedy, the second time as farce."[12] The exact source of Hegel's comments about the compulsive repetition of history remain somewhat obscure, but the influence of Hegel on Marx's historical tropology here is clear.[13] It is clear from his youthful theological essays through the *Phenomenology* to his *Aesthetics* and the *Philosophy of Right*[14] that the Hegelian dialectic with its movement through thesis, antithesis, and synthesis is explicitly connected to Hegel's analysis of tragedy. In the *Phenomenology of Spirit*, Hegel does not so much use Sophocles's *Antigone* to illustrate the dialectical development of the history of spirit as he uncovers the dialectical movement as the essence of tragedy that becomes the master trope for understanding historical progress.

In these passages Marx brings Hegel's tragic dialectic into contact with the latter's aesthetic theories of the evolution of genre. Still, while he follows Hegel's narrative of temporal evolution, he reverses his valuation of the respective genres. For while Hegel's repeated references to tragedy speak to his admiration, he nevertheless places comedy at a higher stage in the development of spirit. Comedy is associated by Hegel with the advent of subjectivity. Subjectivity describes the moment when the self elevates itself above objectivity (the passive adherence to social norms) and achieves a higher state of self-consciousness. Marx, by contrast, clearly sees tragic action as a more *authentic* analogue for the movement of history. In figuring first Germany and then Louis Bonaparte as the comic counterparts to the French revolutionary heroes, he clearly intends to diminish their claim to world-historical significance.[15] Such an implicit hierarchy lies behind his later reference to tragedy in *The Eighteenth Brumaire*:

> But unheroic as bourgeois society is, it nevertheless took the heroism, self-sacrifice, terror, civil war and battles of people to bring it into being. And in the classically austere traditions of the Roman Republic its gladiators found the ideals and the art forms, the self-deceptions that they needed in order to conceal from themselves the bourgeois limitations of the content of their struggles and to keep their enthusiasm on the high plane of the great historical tragedy.[16]

This passage spells out Marx's ultimate disillusionment with the French Revolution of 1789 and the "age of revolutions" that ensued. The "content" of their struggles turned out to be limited to establishing the bourgeoisie rather than delivering on their promise of human emancipation. Yet it was the classical traditions of the Roman Republic and the grandiose form of tragedy that enabled their actors to deceive themselves they were involved in acts of heroism. Louis Bonaparte, by contrast, is involved in a different level of self-deception. Like his more famous uncle, he reaches back to antiquity for an ancient "art form," but instead of tragic heroism he finds debased farce: "Thus the awakening of the dead in those revolutions served the purpose of glorifying the new struggles, not of parodying the old; of magnifying the given task in imagination, not of fleeing from its solution in reality; of finding once more the spirit of revolution, not of making its ghost walk about again."[17]

While the appeal to antiquity in 1789 was an attempt to find "once more the spirit of revolution," in the coup of 1851 it had become an act of necromancy. Marx would return to this same conjunction of historical repetition and dramatic metaphor a third time, in the 1860s. He now turns attention away from the European revolutions to the New World. In a structure that is familiar from *The Eighteenth Brumaire*, Marx compares the advances of the American Revolution to the Emancipation Proclamation issued by Lincoln almost a century later, in 1863. Marx writes in an article in *Die Presse*:

> Lincoln's proclamation is even more important than the Maryland campaign. Lincoln is a *sui generis* figure in the annals of history. He has no initiative, no idealistic impetus, no cothurnus, no historical trappings. He gives his most important actions always the most commonplace form. . . . His latest proclamation, which is drafted in the same style, the manifesto abolishing slavery, is the most important document in American history since the establishment of the Union, tantamount to the tearing up of the old American Constitution.[18]

Unlike the heroes of the French Revolution, Lincoln did not "perform the task of [his] time . . . in Roman costumes and with Roman phrases." He neither looked back to the past to recover the "spirit of the revolution" nor attempted to resurrect the dead. Throwing off the cothurnus of tragedy, he adopts a "commonplace form." He thus eschews the rhetorical trappings of both his European counterparts and the original actors of the American Revolution.[19] Marx continues:

> Nothing is simpler than to show that Lincoln's principal political actions contain much that is aesthetically repulsive, logically inadequate, farcical in form and, politically,

contradictory, as is done by, the English Pindars of slavery, the *Times*, the *Saturday Review* and *tutti quanti*. But Lincoln's place in the history of the United States and of mankind will, nevertheless, be next to that of Washington! Nowadays, when the insignificant struts about melodramatically on this side of the Atlantic, is it of no significance at all that the significant is clothed in everyday dress in the new world? The new world has never achieved a greater triumph than by this demonstration that, given its political and social organisation, ordinary people of good will can accomplish feats which only heroes could accomplish in the old world! Hegel once observed that comedy is in act superior to tragedy and humourous reasoning superior to grandiloquent reasoning. Although Lincoln does not possess the grandiloquence of historical action, as an average man of the people he has its humour.[20]

The "farcical form" of Lincoln's political intervention should not mask the revolutionary content of his actions. By clothing themselves in ancient dress, both the original French revolutionaries and Louis Bonaparte were involved in "self-deception." Yet it was Louis Bonaparte's specifically farcical rather than tragic reenactment that exposed the bad faith of his actions. Lincoln, by contrast, embraces the popular form of comedy while engaging in action at its most authentic. The American Revolution may have shared the "bourgeois limitations" of its French successor, yet, in declaring the end of slavery, Lincoln was involved in a genuine quest for human emancipation.

Marx seems to have a new name for the kind of performance he finds most troubling and insincere: melodrama. Melodrama is the genre that cloaks itself in tragic grandeur but unwittingly becomes farce. It has none of the purity of the two great dramatic genres to emerge from antiquity. It also has none of the ancient pedigree of its generic counterparts. Indeed, as the critic Peter Brooks argues, the "melodramatic imagination" was fundamentally tied up with the experience of modernity.[21] Emerging as a self-conscious genre during the course of the nineteenth century, melodrama, for Marx, spoke to the existential malaise of the Old World. It is all sensation without disruption, the antithesis of the promise of revolution. Melodrama, as Brooks notes, emerged as a genre in France in the aftermath of the Revolution. It is thus in its essence a *postrevolutionary* genre, the generic shrug to the failed tragedy of the Revolution.

In Marx's third use of the theatrical trope, the reference to Hegel's analysis of genre becomes explicit. Staying close to the Hegelian text, he reverses his previous valuation of tragedy and comedy. Lincoln's homespun humor is presented as the true revolutionary answer to old Europe's tragedy. It is comedy's relationship to the people that recasts tragedy as the genre of an outmoded aristocracy. Writing about *The Eighteenth Brumaire*, the literary theorist Peter Stallybrass argues that Marx rejects the status of classical genres *tout court*. "To put it another way, the classical hierarchy of genres, in which tragedy was considered the most elevated and farce the most debased of genres, can no longer retain its unquestioned status within a bourgeois society that pursues the 'novel.' Tragedy must now itself be understood as farce."[22] But rather than rejecting classical genres as such, Marx deploys them strategically, to create a contrast between authentic and inauthentic action. The problem with the Germany of 1843, the problem with the Louis Bonaparte of 1851, and the problem with the Old World of the 1860s were not one of form but of content. Comedy looks like farce in the Old World, but in the New World, where Lincoln is upholding government "of the people, by the people, for the people," it can be returned to its Athenian democratic lineage:

> Men make their own history, but they do not make it just as they please; they do not make it under circumstances

> chosen by themselves, but under circumstances directly encountered, given and transmitted from the past. The tradition of all the dead generations weighs like a nightmare on the brain of the living. And just when they seem engaged in revolutionising themselves and things, in creating something that has never yet existed, precisely in such periods of revolutionary crisis they anxiously conjure up the spirits of the past to their service and borrow from them names, battle cries and costumes in order to present the new scene of world history in this time-honoured disguise and this borrowed language.[23]

In the old Europe, the classical genres of tragedy and comedy can be experienced only as a "borrowed language." Steeped in classical learning and reverence for the past, the European actors experience these "dead generations" as a nightmare. Marx here anticipates Nietzsche's characterization of the historical sense in his *Untimely Meditations*:

> To be sure, we need history. But we need it in a manner different from the way in which the spoilt idler in the garden of knowledge uses it, no matter how elegantly he may look down on our coarse and graceless needs and distresses. That is, we need it for life and action, not for a comfortable turning away from life and action or merely for glossing over the egotistical life and the cowardly bad act. We wish to use history only insofar as it serves living. But there is a degree of doing history and a valuing of it through which life atrophies and degenerates.[24]

Unlike the "insignificant [who] struts about melodramatically on this side of the Atlantic," Lincoln, in Marx's eyes, was unencumbered by tradition, not weighed down by a historical sense.

Yet, it is he who finds "once more the spirit of revolution" and returns history in comic form back to "life and action."

From the 1840s to the 1860s, from Paris to Gettysburg, Marx's understanding of revolutionary action is shot through with dramatic metaphors. Writing half a century after the French Revolution, Marx was able to watch its unfolding as a spectacle. Yet this spectacularization of revolution was not limited to its distant observers. The revolutionaries themselves were aware of the dramatic dimension of their actions. At the heart of the revolutionary theater was the guillotine.[25] The act of beheading was accompanied by a series of self-conscious theatrical devices: the procession of the tumbrel conveying the prisoners, the orchestrated approach to the scaffold, the hush of the crowd, and the display of the severed head. This is how Edmund Burke describes the execution of two of the king's bodyguards in his *Reflections on the Revolution in France*:

> These two gentlemen, with all the parade of an execution of justice, were cruelly and publickly dragged to the block, and beheaded in the great court of the palace. Their heads were stuck upon spears, and led the procession; whilst the royal captives who followed in the train were slowly moved along, amidst the horrid yells, and shrilling screams, and frantic dances, and infamous contumelies, and all the unutterable abominations of the furies of hell, in the abused shape of the vilest women.... Is this a triumph to be consecrated at altars? to be commemorated with grateful thanksgiving? to be offered to the divine humanity with fervent prayer and enthusiastic ejaculation?—These Theban and Thracian Orgies, acted in France, and applauded only in the Old Jewry.[26]

It was this display, this orgy of violence, that lies behind the power of Burke's famous apostrophe to Marie Antoinette:

> It is now sixteen or seventeen years since I saw the queen of France, then the dauphiness, at Versailles; and surely never lighted on this orb, which she hardly seemed to touch, a more delightful vision. . . . Oh, what a revolution! and what a heart must I have, to contemplate without emotion that elevation and that fall! Little did I dream, when she added titles of veneration to those of enthusiastic, distant, respectful love, that she should ever be obliged to carry the sharp antidote against disgrace concealed in that bosom; little did I dream that I should have lived to see such disasters fallen upon her, in a nation of gallant men, in a nation of men of honour, and of cavaliers! I thought ten thousand swords must have leaped from their scabbards, to avenge even a look that threatened her with insult.
>
> But the age of chivalry is gone; that of sophisters, economists, and calculators has succeeded, and the glory of Europe is extinguished forever.[27]

Burke deliberately draws on the Aristotelian discourse of tragedy here. The fall from greatness of a regal individual is the central dynamic of tragic pathos. Yet, as the critic Seamus Deane argues, there is an important contrast that Burke draws "between the natural sympathy felt for her by Burke and the artificial sympathy he would feel were he to see such a scene on stage in a tragedy. The imagery of stripping, nakedness and ruthless ingratitude that dominates his account of the assault on the French queen, and its association of tragic drama, evokes Shakespeare's *King Lear*, a play that operates for some time as a shadow text of the *Reflections*."[28]

Yet the terror brought its own paradox, as the efficiency of the guillotine threatened to eliminate its theatrical potential. In Comay's account of the guillotine, she draws on Michel Foucault's analysis in *Discipline and Punish* to exemplify how the guillotine enacted the transition from "one scopic regime"[29] to another. The guillotine had all the accoutrements of drama but none of its cathartic release. Violence had become so efficient, so mechanized, that it was literally impossible to see the spectacle, let alone be purified by it. As Nicolas Restif de la Bretonne is said to have remarked: "There is no tragedy for them, they don't have *time* to be moved."[30] When Marat boasted to Camille Desmoulins that he "would strike down five hundred, five thousand, twenty thousand in a heartbeat,"[31] Desmoulins responded: "Monsieur Marat . . . you are the dramaturge of journalism; the Danaids, the Barmecides are nothing beside your tragedies. You slit the throat of every character in the play, right down to the prompter. Are you unaware, then, that excess in tragedy goes flat?"[32] The measured grandeur of Greek tragedy has given way to a Senecan celebration of violence. As Comay concludes: "The revolutionary convergence of pity and terror marks the limit of the tragic: at this zero degree of identification, catharsis has become indistinguishable from purge."[33]

In its marrying of theatricalization and violence, the Terror marks the limit point of the Revolution's spectacular politics. During the Terror, the choreography heightens the experience yet simultaneously sanitizes the violence of revolution. Deane writes about Burke's aesthetics that "it is profoundly non-romantic. According to it, no representation can or should compete with the actual. Fables, romances and tragedies have their place, but history and actuality always take precedence over them."[34] For Burke the aesthetics of revolutionary violence merely reveal the decadence of a society that turns to violence in the first place. In contrast to the Romantic aesthetics of a Schlegel who sees the real meaning of revolution in its textualization, Burke's aesthetics decry representation and mandate a return to the actual. However, from Desmoulins to Marx we witness a weariness with spectacle that substitutes for a denunciation of revolutionary violence. There is a desire to be done with theatricalization: to quote Gil Scott-Heron in a new medium with a new genre, "the revolution will not be televised." For as Marx writes of his future communist revolution: "Earlier revolutions required recollections of past world history in order to drug themselves concerning their own content. In order to arrive at its own content, the revolution of the nineteenth century must let the dead bury their dead. There the phrase went beyond the content; here the content goes beyond the phrase."[35] Derrida responds: "No, no more revolutionary memory, down with the monument, bring down the curtain on the shadow theater and funerary eloquence, destroy the mausoleum for popular crowds, shatter the death masks beneath the glass caskets. All of that is the revolution of the past."[36] But as Derrida shows, the problem with theater is not with the *antiquatedness* of its form; it is with form itself:

> But in the future, and already in the *social* revolution of the nineteenth century still to come in Marx's view . . . , the anachrony or untimeliness will not be erased in some plenitude of the parousia and the presence to itself of the present. Time will still be "out of joint." But this time the inadequation will stem from the *excess* of its "own content" with regard to the "phrase." The "own content" will no longer frighten, it will not hide itself, driven back behind the bereaved rhetoric of antique models and the grimace of the death masks. It will exceed the form, it will break out of its clothes, it will overtake signs, models, eloquence, mourning. Nothing there will be any longer an affected mannerism, giving itself airs: no more credit and no more borrowed figure.[37]

The revolutionary actor will need to disrobe, remove his cothurnus, and clad himself in "everyday dress" in order to be true to the content of this new revolution. Lincoln's act of emancipation brings to light the sham emancipation of Europe's bourgeois revolutions. But, even when he "break[s] out of [his] clothes," he merely abandons one ancient form to inhabit another one. Lincoln's authentic act is achieved not by abandoning form but by moving scene and switching genre. The comedy of the New World stands as the solution to the tragedy of the ancien régime.

TRAGEDY AND EMANCIPATION

Liberation is epic, but its aftermaths are tragic.
AIMÉ CÉSAIRE

Marx will turn simultaneously to Hegel's philosophy of history and to his aesthetics to formulate his own theory of revolution, conflating the tragic underpinning of Hegel's account of historical progress with his theory of genres. In Marx's new materialist account of history, the content of the social revolution should be able to exceed its form. Nevertheless, Marx is repeatedly drawn back to Hegel's dramatic emplotment. It is only by changing the scenery, by moving from Europe to America, that form and content will once again be paired. In Lincoln, Marx discovers a comic rather than tragic actor whose revolutionary actions—the abolition of slavery—are the authentic expression of popular comedy.

Marx's focus on Lincoln, however, signals more than a transition from tragedy to comedy. The setting of the New World, along with the question of emancipation itself, opens up a new metaphorical register. In the second half of this chapter, I want to explore what happens to the question of genre as it collides with a different discourse of freedom and insurrection: the slave revolt. We will see how Hegel and Marx continue to shape the conceptual landscape even as their European vantage point is challenged. This section will thus explore the particular tragic bind of "tropical revolution."[38] Focusing on C. L. R. James's account of the Haitian Revolution in *Black Jacobins*, I investigate whether the language of theater and the classical categorization of genre maintain their explanatory power in narrating the hopes and disenchantments of revolutionary actors and their analysts.

In the eighteenth century slavery became a founding metaphor of Enlightenment philosophy. "Yet," as the philosopher Susan Buck-Morss argues, "this political metaphor began to take root at precisely the time that the economic practice of slavery—the systematic, highly sophisticated capitalist enslavement of non-Europeans as a labor force in the colonies—was increasing quantitatively and intensifying qualitatively to the point that by the mid-eighteenth century it came to underwrite the entire economic system of the West, paradoxically facilitating the global spread of the very Enlightenment ideals that were in such fundamental contradiction to it."[39]

If it is Hegel's philosophy of history that gives form to Marx's dialectical materialism, it is his master-slave dialectic that lends it its content. For Hegel, the "struggle to death" between master and slave provides the key to the unfolding of freedom in world history. In asking where Hegel's dialectic originated, scholars have looked to antiquity.[40] For Judith Shklar, the obvious reference is to Aristotle's *Politics* and its discussion of natural slavery (and mastership).[41] In insisting on the reference to ancient slavery and, furthermore, exploring this institution through the philosophical writings of Plato and Aristotle, scholars have conspired to obscure the contemporary in Hegel's writings on slavery. Hegel's slavery is first ancient and then (therefore) abstract and structural. The dual focus on antiquity *and* abstraction ironically finds a parallel in the Marxian reception of the master-slave dynamic. Recall the opening of *The Communist Manifesto*:

> The history of all hitherto existing society is the history of class struggles. Freeman and slave, patrician and plebeian, lord and serf, guild-master and journeyman, in a word, oppressor and oppressed, stood in constant opposition to one another, carried on an uninterrupted, now hidden, now open fight, a fight that each time ended, either in a revolutionary reconstitution of society at large, or in the common ruin of the contending classes.[42]

The ancient Greek freeman and slave who stand at the origin of this power struggle are metamorphosed into the social structures first of Rome, then of medieval Europe, and then of the Renaissance. But what starts out as a *historical* progression soon becomes a *conceptual* progression, as freeman and slave morph into the universal "oppressor and oppressed." "Since the 1840s," writes Buck-Morss, "with the early writings of Karl Marx, the struggle between master and slave has been abstracted from literal reference and read once again as a metaphor—this time for the class struggle."[43] While Marx grounds his response to the *Phenomenology* in a critique of its abstraction, it is Marx's own abstraction of the master-slave dialectic that seals Hegel's alienation from his contemporary moment.

As Buck-Morss observes, the *Phenomenology of Spirit* was "written in Jena in 1805–6 (the first year of the Haitian nation's existence) and published in 1807 (the year of the British abolition of the slave trade)."[44] Despite the insistent focus on antiquity in scholarly discussions of the lordship-and-bondage section, Buck-Morss is certainly not alone in seeing Hegel's philosophy as closely engaged with his own historical moment. To quote the philosopher Chris Arthur: "Hegel was born in 1770 and died in 1831. Thus he lived through the most revolutionary epoch the world had yet seen: the overthrow of the old regime in France, the revolutionary wars of Napoleon, his defeat, the restorations. The fact is that Hegel's philosophy, even at its most abstruse, is in continual dialogue with the real historical movement. Everyone recognises this."[45] If, then, it is commonplace to think of Hegel's philosophy as a reaction to the experience of revolution, the question then becomes, *which* revolution?[46]

In writing about the master-slave dialectic, Buck-Morss argues, Hegel highlights how the struggle for political emancipation in the French Revolution had a parallel in the Haitian slave revolt. In fact, she argues, "Events in Saint-Domingue were central to contemporary attempts to make sense out of the reality of the French Revolution and its aftermath."[47] Far from being an epiphenomenon of the French Revolution, the Haitian slave revolt became a privileged site for working through its hopes and contradictions. Such centrality was achieved, largely, despite rather than because of the French revolutionaries' own efforts. Although the metaphor of slavery was absolutely central to the mantras of the French Revolution, the question of the persistence of actual slavery in its colonies was only half-heartedly addressed in the metropole.

"Man is born free, and everywhere he is in chains": so begins Jean-Jacques Rousseau's *The Social Contract*, first published in 1762.[48] "And yet," Buck-Morss argues, "even Rousseau, patron saint of the French Revolution, represses from consciousness the millions of really existing, European-owned slaves, as he relentlessly condemns the institution."[49] The French colonies were governed by the Code Noir (Black code), which was established under Louis XIV in 1685 and not definitively abolished until 1848. The Code Noir legalized the institution of slavery but also the branding, torture, and killing of slaves who attempted to revolt. For all Rousseau's revulsion from slavery he never mentions the Code Noir.[50] Neither does Denis Diderot, although the condemnation of the slave trade in the *Encyclopédie* was forthright: "Let the colonies be destroyed rather than be cause of so much evil."[51] As C. L. R. James comments: "Such outbursts neither then nor now have carried weight. And wordy attacks against slavery drew sneers from observers which were not altogether undeserved. The authors were compared to doctors who offered to a patient nothing more than invectives against the disease which consumed him."[52]

When we turn to the actors of the French Revolution the picture is equally ambivalent. As the literary critic Srinivas Aravamudan points out, "Jean-Paul Marat's bestseller, *Les chaînes de l'esclavage*, furthered republican aspirations in France. Yet the reputedly radical treatise is remarkable for the ease with which it uses the word *esclavage* to discuss metropolitan politics while it is completely oblivious to the colonial referent of the word, especially—at a moment that was close to the pinnacle of plantation slavery and the slave trade."[53] Meanwhile, Robespierre, aware of the appropriation of the term *esclavage* to describe the domestic situation, used the euphemism "unfree persons" to describe slavery in the colonies. The most prominent antislavery group was the Amis des Noirs (Friends of the blacks), established in 1788. Although it was a small group it included the influential figures Jacques-Pierre Brissot, the Marquis de Condorcet, and Mirabeau. Through their pamphlets and speeches, they succeeded in making the condition of the slaves a subject of debate among the revolutionaries.

After Louis XVI convoked the Estates General, San Dominguan slave proprietors took the novel step of demanding representation. After the Third Estate was locked out of the meeting at Versailles and disbanded to the Tennis Court, the San Dominguans followed them. They were in turn granted representation by the bourgeoisie who feared the economic consequences of their exclusion. Incensed, Mirabeau turned on them: "You claim representation proportionate to the number of inhabitants. The free blacks are proprietors and tax payers, and yet they have not been allowed to vote. And as for the slaves, either they are men or they are not; if the colonists consider them to be men, let them free them and make them electors and eligible for seats; if the contrary is the case, have we, in apportioning deputies according to the population of France, taken into consideration the number of our horses and our mules?"[54] Mirabeau thus exposed the hypocrisy of the racial bias of the fight for freedom. "The unfolding of the logic of freedom in the colonies threatened to unravel the total institutional framework of the slave economy that supported such a substantial part of the French bourgeoisie, whose political revolution, of course this was."[55]

But, rather than the activities of the Amis des Noirs in Paris, it was the actions of the slaves of San Domingo that made the question of slavery central to revolutionary politics. In 1791 half a million slaves organized a violent revolt in San Domingo, the largest and richest French colony. As Aravamudan puts it, "The blacks, slaves themselves, realized that if metaphorical slaves could revolt, literal ones ought not to be left behind."[56] As a result, slavery was abolished on the island in 1793, and a year later the revolutionary government abolished slavery throughout the French colonies. Rather than being the result of proactive campaigning by the Parisian revolutionaries, the abolition came about in response to the events on the ground in the colonies. In fact, the abolition was an emergency measure to prevent the British occupation of the island. In his groundbreaking account of the events in San Domingo, C. L. R. James coined the term *Black Jacobins* to describe the revolting slaves. He thus marks out the intimate connection between the struggle for political emancipation in Paris and the slaves' struggle for literal emancipation in the colonies. It is an irony that the cause of abolition was heavily associated with the Girondin wing of the Revolution, rather than with the Jacobins, who never played an active part in the cause of abolition.[57] In highlighting the slaves' loyalty to the ideals of the Revolution, James's narrative brings to the fore the tragic predicament of their revolution. True to the spirit of that revolution, they found themselves betrayed by its actors.

James's work focuses on the figure of Toussaint-Louverture. Little is known for sure about his childhood and background. He is thought to have been born on the plantation of Bréda. Pierre Baptiste, a freed slave who lived on the plantation, was his godfather and is said to have taught him French and educated him in the European classics. James follows others in attributing Toussaint's political awakening to his early reading of the Abbé Raynal's encyclopedic *Histoire philosophique et politique des établissements et du commerce des Européens dans les deux Indes* (*A Philosophical and Political History of the Settlements and Trade of the Europeans in the East and West Indies*), first published in 1770.[58] James imagines the young Toussaint reading its most famous passage:

> If then, ye nations of Europe, interest alone can exert it's [*sic*] influence over you, listen to me once more. Your slaves stand in no need either of your generosity or your counsels, in order to break the sacrilegious yoke of their oppression. Nature speaks a more powerful language than philosophy, or interests. Already have two colonies of fugitive Negroes been established, to whom treaties and power give a perfect security from your attempts. These are so many indications of the impending storm, and the Negroes only want a chief, sufficiently courageous, to lead them on to vengeance and slaughter.
>
> Where is this great man, whom nature owes to her afflicted,

oppressed, and tormented children? Where is he? He will undoubtedly appear, he will shew himself, he will lift up the sacred standard of liberty. This venerable signal will collect around him the companions of his misfortunes. They will rush on with more impetuosity than torrents; they will leave behind them, in all parts, indelible traces of their just resentment. In all parts the name of the hero, who shall have restored the rights of the human species will be blest; in all parts trophies will be erected to his glory. Then will the black code be no more; and the white code will be a dreadful one, if the conqueror only regards the right of reprisals.[59]

James comments: "Over and over again Toussaint read this passage. . . . A courageous chief was wanted. It is the tragedy of mass movements that they need and can only rarely find adequate leadership."[60] Although the scene of Toussaint reading the so-called "Black Spartacus" passage is probably apocryphal, for James as for others, the debt to the French Enlightenment becomes a cornerstone of the story of Haitian nationalism. As Aravamudan observes: "Whereas in myth the national hero leads his people out of bondage according to a preconceived plan communicated by divine revelation (evident in the abortive rebellions of the Sierra Leone settlers, whose rhetoric harked back to the Exodus), the narrative of the secular nation-state prefers the revolutionary pamphlet as the more acceptable call to arms."[61] But this spectacle of literary epiphany is not represented in altogether triumphalist tones. This is the first of several references to tragedy that punctuate James's account of the Haitian Revolution. For James, what is at stake here is the question of heroism and the relationship between the hero and the masses. Indeed, James will repeatedly return to the language of tragedy to describe the vexed relationship between revolutionary leaders and the people they purport to represent.[62] The echoes with Marx's characterization of Lincoln are strong—one source of the tragedy in his emancipation proclamation was his failure to politically enfranchise the people he spoke for. In an influential argument, the anthropologist David Scott has criticized James for what he calls a "Romantic" notion of historiography—that is to say, an "inclination to privilege the historic role of the heroic personality."[63] Scott draws on Hayden White's distinction between Romantic and tragic modes of historical emplotment. In White's schema, "the Romance is fundamentally a drama of self-identification symbolized by the hero's transcendence over the world of experience, his victory over it, and final liberation from it."[64] Tragedy, like comedy, allows some level of reconciliation between the hero and his environment, but as White suggests, "In tragedy the reconciliations are much more somber; they are more in the nature of the resignations of men to the conditions in which they must labor in the world. These conditions, in turn, are asserted to be inalterable and eternal and the implication is that man cannot change them but must work within them."[65] Toussaint's chosen name, "Louverture" or "L'Ouverture," speaks to Scott's identification of him as a Romantic hero.[66] In his ability to "open up" the future, Toussaint embodies the Arendtian natal.[67] Here we have the myth of a revolution without tragic repetition or comic riff, the promise of a revolution that opens up its own language with no need to recycle the past. No surprise, then, that the figure of Toussaint was heavily lionized by the Romantics and the subject of a sonnet by Wordsworth.

Scott argues that James's perspective on the Haitian Revolution changed between the original publication of *Black Jacobins*, in 1938, and the second edition, of 1963. In particular, he highlights "the new conceptual space [James] assigns to tragedy," which emerges as a result of contemporary historical events and changes in James's own identity. One could also highlight James's deep immersion in Hegel's philosophy in the intervening years.[68] Yet, as the reference above to tragedy shows, even in the first edition there are signs that James is writing in a tragic rather than a Romantic key. The theatrical dimension to the first edition should not surprise us, as James's historiographical classic is actually the reworking of his 1934 play *Toussaint Louverture*.[69] This passage speaks to the Romantic heroism of Toussaint while semantically introducing the vocabulary of tragedy. For James immediately follows the scene of political awakening with a speculation on the dialectic between the individual and the masses, a dialectic that he describes as tragic. More a Greek tragic hero than a Romantic one, Toussaint could not avoid a dialogue with the chorus.

Such a perspective on ancient tragedy was key to James's understanding of the genre. James saw the invention of tragedy as an expression of democratic politics and identified the chorus as representatives of the people.[70] "The tragic hero was a distinguished man. He usually suffered from some weakness—a kind of personal pride to which the Greeks gave a special name—hubris. And any man who sought too much power, too much distinction, to remove himself from the normal, then the tragic destiny was likely to fall upon him. It was a warning to democracy to maintain a certain balance, a certain proportion."[71] As Jeremy Glick writes of James's approach: "Tragedy is a form that speaks to the intermediary role of leadership in framing an agenda for radical transformation."[72] This curtailing of individual agency by the collective is associated by James with the further determinism of economic structures. So James follows this first reference to tragedy in *Black Jacobins* with a broader analysis of historical agency:

> Men make their own history, and the black Jacobins of San Domingo were to make history which would alter the fate of

millions of men and shift the economic currents of three continents. But if they could seize opportunity they could not create it. The slave-trade and slavery were woven tight into the economics of the eighteenth century. Three forces, the proprietors of San Domingo, the French bourgeoisie and the British bourgeoisie, throve on the devastation of a continent and on the brutal exploitation of millions. As long as these maintained an equilibrium the infernal traffic would go on, and for that matter would have gone on until the present day. But nothing however profitable goes on forever. From the very momentum of their own development, colonial planters, French and British bourgeois, were generating internal stresses and intensifying external rivalries, moving blindly to explosions and conflicts which would shatter the basis of their dominance and create the possibility of emancipation."[73]

Deliberately echoing Marx's *Eighteenth Brumaire*, James follows Marx in linking the question of tragedy to the debate about structure and agency in history. Here James takes up a theme he first proposes in his preface to the first edition: "Great men make history, but only such history as it is possible for them to make. Their freedom of achievement is limited by the necessities of their environment."[74] James adds a Marxist materialist dimension to the German idealist reading of tragedy as a conflict between freedom and necessity. In James's historiography of revolution, the dialectic between individual and masses is allied to the tension between individual volition and social determinism. In *The Eighteenth Brumaire*, Marx immediately follows his reflection on the tragic/comic course of history with his observation that the revolutionaries made their own history but not in circumstances of their choosing.[75] He articulates the extent to which individual and even collective actions are scripted in words, languages, and genres that preexist them. For Marx this limitation has a specifically ancient dimension: the classical genre of tragedy, the heroism of Roman republicanism, these are the "tradition of all the dead generations [that] weighs like a nightmare on the brain of the living."

Toussaint's "tropical" revolution experiences another level of curtailment. The Black Jacobins would make their own history but in a language they "borrowed" from the metropole. When this subaltern speaks, he can only speak French. For James this is the specific location of Toussaint's tragic identity: "The defeat of Toussaint in the War of Independence and his imprisonment and death in Europe are universally looked upon as a tragedy. They contain the authentic elements of the tragic in that even at the height of the war Toussaint strove to maintain the French connection as necessary to Haiti in its long and difficult climb to civilisation. . . . His allegiance to the French Revolution and all it opened out for mankind in general and the people of San Domingo in particular, this had made him what he was. But this in the end ruined him."[76] If Toussaint's reading of Raynal inaugurates his entry into European Enlightenment, his confrontation with Napoleon brings it to its tragic denouement.

Toussaint had fought for emancipation as a Jacobin, and yet he was to see himself reenslaved by the French, ending his life in a French prison. When Napoleon came to power, in 1799, he passed a new constitution that declared that the colonies would be subject to special laws. Napoleon initially sent reassurances that he would not reintroduce slavery. Toussaint was keen to reassure Napoleon of his loyalty; at the same time he drew up a constitution for the whole island, which, while falling short of calling for independence, was detrimental to French interests. As a result Napoleon sent an army to San Domingo to restore French authority. Toussaint had to choose between a return to slavery or a San Domingo without France. His vacillations in the ensuing War of Independence are identified by James as his tragic flaw, his hamartia.

Despite the overt reference to Aristotle, James's tragic conception is more Hegelian than Aristotelian. Toussaint's predicament is the personification of tragic conflict. He "embodies a social crisis, the collision of embattled and irreconcilable social forces.... Toussaint embodies the collision of, on the one hand, the old order of slave plantation San Domingo, and on the other, the new order represented by the Enlightenment ideals of revolutionary France."[77] As James's first reference to tragedy in his discussion of leaders and mass movements reveals, Toussaint's tragedy is specifically the tragedy of colonial modernity. It encapsulates both the tension between intellectual elites oriented toward Europe and the people they represent, and the experience of performing the task of their time in a borrowed language. As David Scott concludes: "*The Black Jacobins* is not only about the profound connection between tragedy and modernity for someone like Toussaint Louverture; it is about the ways in which, for someone like Toussaint Louverture, the modern is confronted *as* a tragic condition, a condition in which there are, as James puts it, *only* tragic alternatives."[78]

In describing the tragedy of Toussaint, James invokes the figure of Prometheus.[79] Ever since the publication of Goethe's eponymous poem, in 1789, the figure of Prometheus had been intimately associated with the projects of the Enlightenment and the fight for emancipation. Marx closely identified with Prometheus in his doctoral dissertation. James himself was a great admirer of Aeschylus and turns consistently to him for his paradigm of Greek tragic vision. Is there perhaps something too residually Romantic in the figure of Prometheus to express the tragic condition that James identifies? Hannah Arendt elects a different tragic protagonist in her analysis of revolution. She concludes *On Revolution* (a book now famous for its silence on the Haitian Revolution) by juxtaposing two passages from Sophocles's *Oedipus at Colonus*. The first is the so-called Silenus ode so admired by Nietzsche: "Not to be born prevails over all meaning uttered in words; by far the second-best for life, once it has appeared, is to go as swiftly as possible whence it came."[80] For Arendt, the wisdom of Silenus finds its counterpart in a speech by Theseus, the founder of Athens, and his praise of the redemptive quality of *polis* life. It is the dialectic between these two tragic visions that Arendt sees as key to understanding the dynamics of political engagement. She thus places revolution between Apollo and Dionysos, between natality and fatality. She acknowledges both the unquenchable thirst that motivates the fight for freedom and also the frustrations and failures that attend it. If Scott is right that it was James's disillusionment with the experience of decolonization that made him realize that the script of postcolonial modernity had to be written in a tragic rather than Romantic key, then perhaps we need to look to the aftermath of revolution as well as to its throes. We are back to the temporalities of revolution. In the course of a discussion of their putative slave revolt, Raynal and Diderot discuss the difficulties of restoration. It is in this context that they light upon a different tragic character:

> The conditions faced by the restorer of a corrupt nation are quite different [from those faced by the founder of a new nation]. He is an architect proposing to build on a ruin-filled site; a doctor attempting to cure a gangrenous corpse; a sage preaching reform to hardened sinners. The restorer can only hope to receive the hatred and the persecution of the present generation, and will not see future ones. He will bear little fruit with much labor during his life, eliciting only sterile regret after his death. A nation can regenerate itself only through a bloodbath, much like the old Aeson, whom

Medea could rejuvenate only by flaying and boiling him. When the nation declines, no man can set it right.. That will be the outcome of a long series of revolutions. The man of genius disappears quickly, leaving no legacy behind.[81]

In a brilliant analysis, Aravamudan proposes a different fictional scene of literary revelation to juxtapose with the canonical episode of Toussaint reading Raynal's "Black Spartacus" passage. "Could we fantasize," he writes, "that Toussaint's 'daughter-in-law,' let us say a domestic servant at the same plantation in Bréda, now reads attentively?"[82] The passage describes events surrounding the character of Medea from book 7 of Ovid's *Metamorphoses*. After capturing the Golden Fleece, Jason and Medea return to Thessaly to find Aeson, Jason's father, on the brink of death. At Jason's request Medea agrees to rejuvenate her father-in-law. Ovid describes the elaborate preparations that Medea made for this act of transformation, seeking out herbs and potions far and wide and performing intricate rituals and libations:

> They retired as she had bidden. Medea, with streaming hair after the fashion of the Bacchantes, moved round the blazing altars, and dipping many-cleft sticks in the dark pools of blood, she lit the gory sticks at the altar flames. Thrice she purified the old man with fire, thrice with water, thrice with sulphur.
> Meanwhile the strong potion in the bronze pot is boiling, leaping and frothing white with the swelling foam.[83]

He then goes on to describe Medea's act of sorcery:

> When she saw this, Medea unsheathed her knife and cut the old man's throat; then, letting the old blood all run out, she

filled his veins with her brew. When Aeson had drunk this in part through his lips and part through the wound, his beard and hair lost their hoary grey and quickly became black again; his leanness vanished, away went the pallor and the look of neglect, the deep wrinkles were filled out with new flesh, his limbs had the strength of youth. Aeson was filled with wonder, and remembered that this was he forty years ago. Now Bacchus had witnessed this marvel from his station in the sky.[84]

Medea revives her father-in-law by cutting his throat and transfusing him with her rich elixir. In the Diderot-Raynal passage this scene of restorative "flaying" is overlaid with a later scene where Medea tricks the daughters of Aeson's treacherous brother, Pelias, into performing the same act on their father.[85] Medea spurs the daughters into dismembering their father and then picks up his dying corpse and immerses it in boiling water. Diderot and Raynal are attentive to the ultimate failure of Medea's action, as she eventually loses the loyalty of Jason that had been her ultimate objective. By analogy, they seem to be arguing that no act of sorcery can ultimately succeed in rejuvenating a moribund state. As Aravamudan comments: "As Medea ultimately failed, an individual agent—man or woman—cannot succeed in restoring the nation, whether by sorcery or surgery; agency has passed into the sphere of collective sociocultural transformations (*une longue suite de révolutions*)."[86] Medea thus embodies the tragic aftermath of the Romantic Prometheus. She is the Bacchus to Toussaint's Apollo, tearing asunder the *principium individuationis* in a violent *sparagmos* of the body politic. "Medea [is] akin to the Derridean *pharmakon, pharmakeus,* and *pharmakos*. Medea is a female agent who can be restorative drug and unbearable poison, the sorcerer and ultimately the sacrificial scapegoat for the rejuvenation of the body politic."[87]

When revolution is narrated as tragedy, Prometheus, Oedipus, and Medea each gives us a different version of the narration. Moreover, in the chronology of revolution, its different stages seem to elicit different formal expressions. Recalling James's claim that Haiti represented "one of the great epics of revolutionary struggle and achievement,"[88] Aimé Césaire observed: "Liberation is epic, but its aftermaths are tragic."[89] The Medea episode highlighted by Diderot and Raynal reverses this chronology. They look to Ovid's epic rather than to Euripides's tragedy to discover a Medea who signifies the difficulties of restoring the body politic after the throes of revolution. Her failure can, in the end, only produce the need for more revolution, for a constant cycle of violence and bloodshed. This is the wisdom of Ovid's *satirical* epic. As Hayden White reminds us, satire ultimately stands against the genres of romance, tragedy, and comedy, discovering only meaningless change in the world: "The archetypal theme of Satire is the precise opposite of [the] Romantic drama of redemption: it is, in fact, a drama of diremption, a drama dominated by the apprehension that man is ultimately a captive of this world rather than its master and by the recognition that, in the final analysis, human consciousness and will are always inadequate to the task of overcoming definitively the dark force of death."[90]

Marx thought that by turning away from Europe to the New World he could leave behind tragic bourgeois revolutions and discover a comedy of human emancipation. Assessing the aftermath of Lincoln's emancipation proclamation, W. E. B. Du Bois could only discover "tragedy that beggared the Greek."[91] Scott traces a postcolonial awareness in James that Romantic struggles of emancipation contain the seeds of their tragic aftermaths. Tragedy and emancipation are inextricably linked. But unlike the satirical vision of history sketched out by White, this "tragedy of emancipation is not a tragedy of *repetition*, of the painful revelation of the unsurpassable limits of human action and the stubbornness of our ambitions, but a tragedy of *novelty*—of the novelty of emancipation as it intersects with . . . the 'profound motion and tragically persistent patterns regarding race.'"[92] Tragedy, as the Greeks knew, is the genre of transition. It is the genre that came to life when the Athenians endeavored to express the novelty of their social and political structures in their difficult confrontation with the old. In this sense, it is Greek tragedy's bifurcated temporality that makes it such a potent trope in the narrativization of modern revolution. The Athenian tragedians are like Marx's revolutionaries, who "just as they seem to be engaged with revolutionizing themselves and things, creating something that has never yet existed, . . . anxiously conjure up the spirits of the past to their service."[93] Oedipus's tragedy would be nothing more than the confrontation of the ancien régime with the new world order. It is the realization of novelty that produces anxiety. Tragedy's philosophy is, in Nietzsche's phrase, the "dangerous perhaps."[94] In thinking about tragedy and revolution, perhaps we ought to shift our understanding of "tragedy from the register of spectacular defeat, and of collective *sacrifice*, to that of patient critique."[95]

Fraternity

ALL MEN WILL HAVE BEEN BROTHERS

In the summer of 1789, the Comte de Mirabeau proclaimed a new era: "History all too often has recounted nothing but the actions of ferocious beasts, among whom on rare occasions it recognises heroes. We have reason to hope that with us begins the history of men, of brothers."[1] We saw in the first chapter how the French revolutionaries would try—and fail—to change the meaning of time itself with the introduction of the Republican calendar. Against the background of an increasing self-consciousness about history and its memorialization, Mirabeau announces a new moment: the age of brothers. Mirabeau's equation of mankind with brotherhood would act as a powerful motor of revolutionary change. While the preceding chapter explored how classical genres molded the modern historiography of revolution, this one explores how the representation of ancient brothers underpinned the revolutionary ideology of fraternity.

Jacques-Louis David's *Oath of the Horatii* (figure 7) sits at the threshold of Mirabeau's historiography. It was first painted by David in Rome in 1784 and displayed to great acclaim at the French Salon (the official exhibition of the Académie des Beaux-Arts) in 1785. The painting was commissioned by an assistant to none other than Louis XVI, and the generous commission allowed David to relocate to Rome. The image draws on

FIGURE 7. Jacques-Louis David, *The Oath of the Horatii*, 1784–85. Musée du Louvre, Paris. Digital image: Peter Horree / Alamy Stock Photo.

the story of early Rome's conflict with Alba Longa, recounted in book 1 of Livy's *History of Rome*. The two cities decide to send three men to go into battle to spare the whole population from going to war. Three triplet brothers from a Roman family, the Horatii, agree to end the war by fighting three brothers from a family of Alba Longa, the Curiatii. David's picture shows the three Roman brothers stepping forward while their father holds swords out for them. Their upright stance represents their willingness to sacrifice their lives for the good of Rome. Only one of the brothers survives the initial confrontation, but this brother kills all three Curiatii. In the bottom-right corner, David represents several women crying. In the foreground is Camilla, a sister of the Horatii brothers, who is engaged to one of the Curiatii fighters. She recognizes that whatever the outcome she will lose one of her loved ones. In fact, Camilla will herself later be killed by her brother for her excessive grief at the death of her future husband. Although Livy's account is the most dramatic, the story also appears in Plutarch and Dionysius of Halicarnassus and it had more recently been retold in the play *Horace* (1640), by Pierre Corneille.[2] A prominent scene in Corneille's play involved the later trial of Camilla's brother for her murder and the rousing plea made on his behalf by his father. The father defends the honor of the brother against the sentimentality of the sister. We know from sketches that David had originally intended to depict this scene inspired by Corneille but decided against it—purportedly because the depiction of a law court speech was too static for visual representation.[3]

The exact source of the scene that David eventually chose is unknown (though this has not stopped critics from speculating). It seems likely that it is his own invention.[4] The same uncertainty surrounds the meaning of David's choice. That the painting showed *aesthetic* radicalism is beyond doubt. As the historian Simon Schama writes: "The painting was like nothing anyone had ever seen: a revolution in art well before David had anything to do with revolution in the state."[5] The austere classicism, the shallowness of the scene, the asymmetrical positioning of the figures, the repeated patterns of three, the closed composition—all of these features made David's painting a sensation. David had self-consciously violated the terms of his royal commission. Given strict instructions on size, he rejected these, vocally defending his decision to enlarge the scale of the work. It was also delivered late to the Salon—a bold move, given the unrivaled role of the exhibition in adjudicating the status and success of artists at the time. David was so keen to make a splash there that he even planted a rumor that he had been killed on his journey back from Rome, only to then make a surprise appearance. His ruse worked and the Salon was forced to extend its viewing hours just to accommodate the popular response to his painting.

For some, such as the art historian Thomas Crow, the painting heralds the political radicalism of the revolutionary-era David.[6] Reactions after its first display suggest that the image was interpreted by some critics as being hostile to the ancien régime—yet, as Schama notes, it is not clear whether these critics are responding to its stylistic or political polemicism. While the painting depicts a great scene of Roman patriotism, it also appears to represent the philosophical ideals of the Enlightenment. Indeed, critics have argued that it specifically alludes to Rousseau's social contract and the republican concept of the general will. The oath sworn by the brothers can be read as an act of unification of men to the binding of the state.[7] The stark division between the male and female characters might also be a reference to Rousseau's discussion of separate spheres for men and women in *Émile*. So this painting may be one part Livy and one part Rousseau. But beyond the direct reference to Rousseau, it has been argued that David's painting is a potent symbol of a new model of patriotism, where allegiance is sworn to the public good rather than to church or king.

Certainly, David's disregard of the specifications of the royal commission and his prodigious success at the Salon changed the nature of the artist's allegiance. As Schama phrases it: "Henceforth he would make pictures for something called 'The Nation.'"[8] Nevertheless, David at this stage in his career was not known to hold subversive political views. As the work was painted some five years before the events that would turn David into a staunch supporter of republicanism, the retrospective attribution of revolutionary intent has been much criticized.[9]

The question of the painting's political *intention*, then, remains moot, yet the radicalism of its impact and reception is beyond doubt. The picture's representation of three *brothers* declaring an oath to Rome certainly lent itself to its post hoc absorption into David's revolutionary canon. The painting's resonance with the ideal of fraternity was, of course, particularly striking. As Mona Ozouf writes: "In the triad of abstractions that compose what Pierre Leroux calls 'the holy motto of our fathers,' fraternity—last and least—is the poor relation."[10] Whereas liberty and equality were ideas with rigorous theorizations in the history of political thought, and in Enlightenment thought more specifically, fraternity was more nebulous. Despite Mirabeau's early championing, fraternity was actually a late addition to the Declaration of the Rights of Man and of the Citizen—it was introduced into official language in a supplementary article to the Constitution of 1791, which, as Ozouf argues, "envisioned fraternity as a remote product of future national holidays. Those holidays were instituted in order to 'foster' fraternity, which was thought of as the goal of a long-term project to shape the civic project and not at all as an immediate objective."[11] Far from a specific turning point in history, as Mirabeau suggests, the "age of brothers" was rather a quasi-messianic hope for the future.

The term *brother* itself, of course, had theological resonances. It was the form of address used by monks and had much wider resonances within Christian discourse. Just as the Republican calendar retained a theological structure while proclaiming its secularism, revolutionary fraternity dressed an old Christian virtue in new secular garb. Differentiating Christianity from Judaism, Matthew (23:8) declares: "But you are not to be called 'Rabbi,' for you have one Teacher, and you are all brothers." At stake in the Christian idea that, as children of God, we are all brothers is the notion of universality.[12] Yet, this universality that transcended notions of tribe and status was predicated on a community of faith. Like so many universalisms, it turns out on closer scrutiny to be particular, too.[13]

Christian fraternity distanced itself from what it cast as the ethnocentrism of Judaism, but also sought to differentiate itself from the classical notion of political *philia*. For Plato in the *Republic*, "All of you in the city are brothers." The civic ties would not only exist side by side with familial ones but would also in some senses transcend them. Plato's blurring of the distinction between the *oikos* and the *polis* is to an extent symptomatic of the priority of the public sphere in Greek thought more generally. Yet the presence of this phrase in the context of the noble lie is surely significant:

> While all of you in the city are brothers, we will say in our tale, yet God in fashioning those of you who are fitted to hold rule mingled gold in their generation, for which reason they are the most precious—but in the helpers silver, and iron and brass in the farmers and other craftsmen. And as you are all akin, though for the most part you will breed after your kinds.[14]

Platonic brotherhood, here, is not only recognized as a fiction, but it is specifically the egalitarian ideal of brotherhood that is not sooner broached than discredited. You may all be brothers "in the city," but such a status does not confer equal status. There is a politics to this political fraternity. This brotherhood may instill solidarity in the city, but it is allied to a highly differentiated idea of the social realm.

Plato's position in the *Republic* thus stands in opposition to the specifically democratic conflation of familial and civic ties through the Athenian myth of autochthony. Ironically, it is Plato's own *Menexenus* where the myth's outlines are most compellingly presented:

> And the cause of this our polity lies in our equality of birth. For whereas all other States are composed of a heterogeneous collection of all sorts of people, so that their polities

also are heterogeneous, tyrannies as well as oligarchies, some of them regarding one another as slaves, others as masters; we and our people, on the contrary, being all born of one mother, claim to be neither the slaves of one another nor the masters; rather does our natural birth-equality drive us to seek lawfully legal equality, and to yield to one another in no respect save in reputation for virtue and understanding.[15]

Here in her funeral oration to Pericles, Aspasia, through the mouth of Socrates, explains the basis of civic equality in Athens. As all Athenians are born from "one mother," the earth, their birth-equality determines their political equality. Since Homer, the Athenians had been considered the sons of the "earth-born" Erechtheus, the legendary founder of the city. Erechtheus was conceived when Athena wiped some of Hephaestus's semen from her thigh on a piece of wool that she dropped to the earth, Gaia, who then became pregnant. The myth of Athens's origins, then, on the one hand, served to cement Athenians' unique relationship to their land; on the other, it naturalized their political organization based on equality. In the *Menexenus*, the fraternal bond is invoked precisely in order to explain the uniqueness of Athenian civic organization—if this fraternity is based on equality, it is certainly *not* based on universality. As Nicole Loraux argued so forcefully, the premise of the myth is exclusion; while the fraternity of civic bonds is established, the myth is predicated on the marginalization of women and foreigners from the political family of Athens.[16] Since male citizenship is conferred by connection to an original "earth" mother, this nullifies the role of human mothers in the production of legitimate citizens: "For it is not the country that imitates the woman in the matter of conception and birth, but the woman the country."[17] The subordination of human mothers to the primal earth mother provided the justificatory framework for a rough male equality but also for the denial of political and civic rights to the real female inhabitants of the city. The ethnocentric basis of myth was also key to its appeal:

> Now as regards nobility of birth, their first claim thereto is this—that the forefathers of these men were not of immigrant stock, nor were these their sons declared by their origin to be strangers in the land sprung from immigrants, but natives sprung from the soil living and dwelling in their own true fatherland; and nurtured also by no stepmother, like other folk, but by that mother-country wherein they dwelt, which bare them and reared them and now at their death receives them again to rest in their own abodes.[18]

There was nothing arbitrary about the Athenians' relationship to their land. By invoking a maternal relationship, the myth established the most secure bond possible between *Blut und Boden*. This context perhaps makes sense of the delay, which we tracked earlier in the book, of French revolutionaries in accepting Jews and the San Dominguans as brothers. Yet, such myths of autochthony, as Derrida argues in *The Politics of Friendship*, are merely a working through of a broader connection between political and familial discourses:

> The concept of politics rarely announces itself without some sort of adherence of the State to the family, without what we call a *schematic* of filiation: stock, genus or species, sex (*Geschlecht*), blood, birth, nature, nation—autochthonal, or not, tellurian or not. This is once again the abyssal question of *phúsis*, the question of being, the question of what appears in birth, in opening up, in nurturing or growing, in producing by being produced....
> If no dialectic of the State ever breaks with what it super-

cedes [*relève*] and from which it arises [*ce dont elle relève*] (the *life* of the family and civil society), if politics never reduces within itself this adherence to familial generation, if any republican motto almost always associates fraternity with equality and freedom, as for democracy, it is rarely determined in the absence of confraternity or brotherhood.[19]

It is the conception of *phúsis* (nature) that Derrida invokes in this passage that underpins Aristotle's account of the emergence of the city in book 1 of the *Politics*. There the *polis* is seen as the development of the partnership of the *oikos* (1252b). While, in Aristotle's terms, the city is prior ("*proteron*," 1253a) to the household, this conceptual priority is a corollary of their fundamental interdependence. This thinking of the *polis* inevitably ties Aristotle to a familial discourse of politics, a familial politics that "so regularly comes back on stage with the features of the *brother* . . . [and] seems spontaneously to belong to a *familial, fraternalist* and thus *androcentric* configuration of politics."[20] But as the *Menexenus* shows, it is a specifically *democratic* politics that seems particularly drawn to the sibling configuration:

> Democracy has seldom represented itself without the possibility of at least that which it always resembles—if one is willing to nudge the accent of this word—the possibility of *fraternization*. The fratriarchy may *include* cousins and sisters but, as we will see, including may also come to mean neutralizing.[21]

There is no democracy, ancient or modern, Derrida seems to assert, without fratriarchy (though, it may be worth noting, the Greek *phratry* was not a specifically democratic mode of organization).[22] The brotherly relation in its horizontality rejects the hierarchical encoding of monarchical constitutions. Derrida is aware that in citing the *Menexenus* as evidence of a Greek configuration of political thought ("a goldmine of commonplaces")[23] he is dealing with a text whose tone remains difficult to determine.[24] Can we imagine Socrates's position as he repeats the praise of democracy from the mouth of Aspasia herself, mimicking Pericles's funeral oration, to be anything other than ironic? Derrida calls the *Menexenus* "a fiction-in-fiction," but this tricky narrative framing mirrors a deeper thematic fictionality:

> A genealogical tie will never be simply real... it is... a "legal fiction," as Joyce put it in *Ulysses* on the subject of paternity.... Everything in political discourse that appeals to birth, to nature or to the nation—indeed, to nations or to the universal nation of human brotherhood—this entire familialism consists in a renaturalization of this "fiction." What we are calling here "fraternization," is what produces symbolically, conventionally, through authorized engagement, a *determined politics*, which, be it left- or right-wing, alleges a real fraternity or regulates spiritual fraternity, fraternity in the figurative sense, on the symbolic projection of a real or natural fraternity. Has anyone ever met a brother? A uterine and consanguine (distantly related) brother? In nature?[25]

So while the elective relationship of citizens in a *polis* yearns to be underpinned by a natural affiliation, this relationship "in nature" turns out itself to be highly conventional. Natural fraternity seeks to recode *nomos* (law) as *phúsis*; but as Joyce—and Homer—remind us, there is nothing natural about familial relations.

Thinking through the position of the friend in the history of political thought, Derrida highlights the role of the French Revolution in foregrounding a familial politics of democracy. Derrida's argument is that the tendency—with profound roots in Greco-Roman thought—to analogize the political sphere to the family has lasting consequences for our understanding of the limits of citizenship. In the concept of fraternity, the French Revolution would bring together the emphasis on natural kinship of the civic community found in Greek thought with the appeal to universalism that subtends the Christian rhetoric of brotherhood. A more implicit dimension of Derrida's critique is the way the French Revolution, through its classical imagery and rhetoric, enshrines a fraternal relationship to antiquity. The classicization of brotherhood is also the fraternization of the classics, with consequences for the shape of revolutions to come. The ancients are an elective family masquerading as a natural one. And this natural filiation prevents us from conceiving other elective affinities in a future politics.

In its formulation of a protodemocratic vision of politics, the revolutionary ideal of *fraternité* would become synonymous with the Western liberal conception of the state.[26] So much is clear, as Stefani Engelstein notes, from the European Union's decision to choose as its anthem the final movement of Beethoven's Ninth Symphony, which sets to music Friedrich Schiller's "Ode to Joy": "The poem 'Ode to Joy' expresses Schiller's idealistic vision of the human race becoming brothers—a vision Beethoven shared. There are no words to the anthem. In the universal language of music, this anthem expresses the European ideals of freedom, peace and solidarity."[27] Although, in its flight from words, the language of music may be "universal," it is clearly Schiller's phrase "Alle Menschen werden Brüder" that lies behind the choice of the anthem. And while the website states that Beethoven set to music "Friedrich von Schiller's lyrical verse from 1785," the specific line was a revision by Schiller in his 1805 version. The belatedness of Schiller's reference to brotherhood thus mirrors the ex post facto interpretation of David's 1785 painting as an embodiment of the revolutionary ideal of *fraternité*. Untimeliness appears to be a feature of fraternity. Moreover, as Engelstein argues, the easy elision between "universalism" and "European ideals" is just one of the complexities of this choice: "The connection between brotherhood and freedom comes across as self-evident, enshrined as it is in the familiar slogan of the French Revolution, *Liberté, Egalité, Fraternité*. Like the ode and the French rallying cry, however, the EU web text manifests a series of paradoxes in the understanding of fraternity."[28] For while the revolutionary tricolon appears to hold together, it actually pulls in different directions:

> The fraught ideal of fraternity reveals a series of ideological struggles within the three terms of the revolutionary motto. The concept of liberal democracy, a political organization governed by liberty and equality, was built on a foundation of newly conceived subjects. As free individuals, such self-interested subjects could be assumed to compete and create strife in the polis. The rhetoric of equality, on the other hand, draws subjects rather toward similitude, challenging the growing validation of the individual. The byword of universal brotherhood serves to balance these opposing forces. On the one hand, it tempers self-interest by evoking the affective investments of individuals and redirecting them toward the general good; on the other, fraternity alleviates the abstract similitude of equals through a dynamic that preserves particularistic desire safely by projecting it, and hence its objects, into a realm outside politics. Fraternity thus creates the domestic sphere and polices its boundaries, channeling the exclusive ties of passion and kinship toward the nation.[29]

Brotherhood thus provides both the glue and the spur to dissolution of the relationship between liberty and equality. It tempers their opposing tendencies and displaces the site of conflict beyond the political sphere. Yet, this image of brotherhood as a source of reconciliation seems at odds with both the lived reality and the mythologization of the sibling bond. Eteocles and Polynices, Romulus and Remus, Moses and Aaron, Cain and Abel, Isaac and Ishmael, Jacob and Esau—these are the brothers we associate with the foundation of cities and peoples. As Jean-Luc Nancy writes: "The motif of the *enemy brothers* plays a key role in all kinds of mythologies. We ordinarily understand it as pointing to a kind of moral monstrosity, but it actually speaks the simple truth of a relation that is erratic and astray, indeed insane."[30]

Despite Nancy's claim, such fraternal conflict is not usually seen as monstrous. In the Hebrew Bible, in particular, "The theme of sibling rivalry is achingly familiar, winding its violent way through the entire primeval and ancestral history of Israel."[31] In the biblical context, moreover, primogeniture ensures that fraternal equality is exposed as a phantasm ab initio. No doubt it is this association of brotherhood with the worst excesses of competitive masculinity that will persuade a figure like Nancy of the need to move beyond fraternity: "It would no doubt be better to refer to 'sorority,' granting that the fraternal does privilege a masculine one-sidedness. Sorority would be fraternity beyond or below the law."[32] Nevertheless, the appeal of a sisterhood "beyond or below the law" mirrors rather than undoes the idiom of brotherhood that always invites a depoliticization at the same time as it grounds political rhetoric. A sisterhood beyond the law negates both the extent to which the law has actively policed the exclusion of women and the potential for "sorority" itself to name a site of conflict:

> The fratriarchy may *include* cousins and sisters but, as we will see, including may also come to mean neutralizing.

Including may dictate forgetting, for example, with "the best of all intentions," that the sister will never provide a docile example for the concept of fraternity. This is why the concept must be rendered docile, and there we have the whole of political education. What happens when, in taking up the case of the sister, the woman is made a sister? And a sister a case of the brother? This could be one of our most insistent questions, even if, having done so too often elsewhere, we will here avoid convoking Antigone, here again the long line of history's Antigones, docile or not, to this history of brothers that has been told to us for thousands of years.[33]

In his reading of *Antigone*, Hegel famously considered the brother-sister relationship to be the paradigmatic ethical relationship. Circumventing all the ironies of the Oedipal legacy, Hegel insists that the relationship between Antigone and Polynices is one without desire, which allows the sister to transcend the natural limitations of her sex. Hegel's analysis, therefore, doubles down on the Sophoclean passage considered most problematic by his peers.[34] Yet in the context of the ideology of *fraternité*, this looks less like a Hegelian idiosyncrasy. The premise of Antigone's argument, in fact, speaks to a particular trait of revolutionary fraternity:

> For never, had children of whom I was the mother or had my husband perished and been mouldering there, would I have taken on myself this task, in defiance of the citizens. In virtue of what law do I say this? If my husband had died, I could have had another, and a child by another man, if I had lost the first, but with my mother and my father in Hades below, I could never have another brother.[35]

Antigone characterizes the brother as the locus of parental absence. While, contra Hegel, it is tempting to see Antigone's attachment to her brother as the compulsion to repeat the incest of her parents, it is also necessary to acknowledge the singularity of their bond—a singularity that is predicated on the loss of her father. The irreplaceability of the brother (*fraternity/sorority*) is a function of the death of the father (and the mother). Encoded in Antigone's name (*Anti-gone* = anti-generation) is the rejection of the patrilineal in favor of a queer (fraternal) futurity.[36]

WE BAND OF BROTHERS

*The figure or the sign of the father, and consequently of fraternity as well, offers an empty space [*la vacance*] that must be filled in one way or another. Brothers are originally orphans who have lost their father, such that nothing allows us to identify them as being associated through whatever it may be—unless it is through the absorption of maternal nourishment, which leads to their emancipation. From the moment that the paternal vacuum [*vacance paternelle*]—the "power vacuum" [*vacance du pouvoir*] as it is called within the socio-political order—is manifested as such, one must confront the obvious truth that can no longer be concealed by any foundational mythology (a function that is always imperfectly fulfilled, regardless of the mythology). This is the lot of democracy: it must take on this vacuum without appealing to a mythology.*

JEAN-LUC NANCY, "FRATERNITY"

Lynn Hunt argues that "most Europeans in the eighteenth century thought of their rulers as fathers and of their nations as families writ large."[37] Such a vision of power goes back to antiquity: in the first book of the *Politics*, Aristotle may question the analogy between the political leader and the head of the household but he still asserts: "The relationship of father to sons is regal in type, since a father's first care is for his children's welfare.... The ideal of kingship is paternal government."[38] In Rome, meanwhile, the senate had the power to confer the honor of *pater patriae* on its leaders—republican and imperial alike. The French revolutionary era, as Hunt outlines, would shift the model of power from a vertical, patrilineal model of power to a horizontal one:

> Kingship was officially abolished on 21 September 1792. Deputy Henri Grégoire explained, "It's necessary to destroy this word *king*, which is still a talisman whose magical force can serve to stupefy many men." In January 1793 the man Louis Capet [Louis XVI] himself was executed. The killing of the political father enacted a ritual sacrifice and opened the way to the band of brothers. Between 1792 and the middle of 1794, radical iconography instantiated a new family romance of fraternity: brothers and sisters appeared frequently in this iconographic outpouring, mothers rarely, and fathers almost never. The literal effacement of the political father was the subject of a systematic, official campaign in which images of the kings of France, as well as images of royalty, aristocracy, and feudalism, were destroyed.[39]

Kingship gives way to a new model of kinship. The iconography of revolution would shift its focus to a new family romance. But, as Hunt further suggests, the response to the killing of the king in France was ambivalent. Much of the press reported the event in a sober, restrained fashion and there was no call for general celebration. By contrast, in more radical circles, figures such as Marat would compare the execution to a "religious festival": "One would have said that [the people] had just attended a religious festival; delivered from the burden of oppression that weighed on them for such a long time and pierced by the sentiment of fraternity, all hearts gave themselves over to the hope of a happier future."[40] The aftermath of regicide was thus likened by Marat to a spiritual ritual "pierced by . . . fraternity." Louis Prudhomme, writing in the paper *Révolutions de Paris*, would further develop the language of sacrificial ritual. In Hunt's account: "When describing the scene at the scaffold after the execution and the benediction of the 'brothers' with the king's blood, Prudhomme recounted the complaint of a witness, who feared the assimilation of the scene with cannibalism: 'My friends, what are we doing? All of this is going to be reported; they are going to paint us abroad as a ferocious and bloodthirsty mob.' A defiant voice responded: 'Yes, thirsty for the blood of a despot; let them go retell it, if you like, to everyone on earth.'"[41] The republic, for Prudhomme, is consummated by the devouring of the king. It is difficult not to see in Marat's and Prudhomme's descriptions a prefiguring of Sigmund Freud's discussion of the "totem meal" in *Totem and Taboo*. The festival atmosphere is famously connected by Freud to the ur-act of patricide:

> If we call the celebration of the totem meal to our help, we shall be able to find an answer. One day the brothers who had been driven out came together, killed and devoured their father and so made an end to the patriarchal horde. United, they had the courage to do and succeeded in doing what would have been impossible for them individually. . . . The violent primal father had doubtless been the feared and envied model of each one of the company of brothers: and in the act of devouring him they accomplished their identification with him, and each one acquired a portion of his strength. The totem meal, which is perhaps mankind's earliest festival, would be a repetition and a commemoration of this memorable criminal deed, which was the beginning

of so many things—of social organisation, of moral restrictions and religion."[42]

The primal horde who unseat the father and commit the first act of patricide, in Freud's version, are also ultimately responsible for bringing in a new world order. For Freud, "social organisation" and "morality" arise as a guilt response to an initial act of unguarded violence. The brothers' act is therefore responsible for initiating civilization, as such: "They thus created out of their filial sense of guilt the two fundamental taboos of totemism, which for that reason inevitably corresponded to the two repressed wishes of the Oedipus Complex."[43] The prohibitions against murder and incest enact a transformation of the social organization *and* a revolution in thought. "The age of brothers," as Mirabeau had hoped, is thus truly a turning point in history. While for Freud the family drama becomes a motor of social change, the reverse dynamic would take place in France. As Balzac would write, "By cutting off the head of Louis XVI, the Republic cut off the head of all the fathers of families."[44] The events in the political sphere would have an impact on the structure of family, and several laws were passed by deputies in the National Convention that diminished the power of fathers over their children.[45] Politics had changed the meaning of fatherhood and showed the dependence of family on the state, and not just vice versa.

The triumph of the brothers over the dead father stands in contrast to David's earlier depiction of fraternity. In *The Oath of the Horatii*, David celebrates the fraternal bond in the *presence* of the father; indeed it is the paternal prerogative to exhort his sons to heroism. Even in the later painting *Lictors Bring to Brutus the Bodies of His Sons* (1789), which so ominously foretells the slaying of the king, the father takes center stage in a reversal that will see the patriarch murder the brothers in the name of the republic. A reminder, perhaps, that the story of Oedipus starts with an attempted *filicide*. In Bonnie Honig's reading of the *Bacchae* it is a band of sisters who conspire to kill the royal *son*.[46] Recalling not just the story of Oedipus but that of Isaac and Jesus, too, Silke-Maria Weineck argues that "the fantasies of patricide and filicide are inextricably linked."[47]

The American Revolution drew inspiration from many of the same ancient Greco-Roman sources. The Declaration of Independence was signed in Philadelphia, the city of brotherly love, yet the revolutionaries seem not to have envisaged their society as postpaternal. Although the relationship between Britain and America was understood through the framework of familial relations, with the colonial sons in revolt against an "unnatural father," during the War of Independence the brothers reached maturity, and "in 1778 Washington was referred to for the first time as 'the Father of His Country.'"[48] The rhetoric of founding fathers would coexist with an ideology of freedom and equality. While the American model may appear to stand in contrast to the French revolutionary experience, its example perhaps speaks rather to the inevitable transience of the fratriarchy (and, given the coming civil war, depicted as a war between brothers, fratricide, too). Here is Freud:

> Thus after a long lapse in time their bitterness against the father, which had driven them to their deed, grew less, and their longing for him increased; and it became possible for an ideal to emerge which embodied the unlimited power of the primal father against whom they had once fought as well as their readiness to submit to him. As a result of decisive cultural changes, the original democratic equality that had prevailed among all the individual clansmen became untenable; and there developed at the same time an inclination ... to revive the ancient paternal ideal.[49]

For Freud, the period of "original democratic equality" inaugurated by the act of patricide is ultimately "untenable." The same feelings of aggression that were formerly directed against the father erupt between the brothers. And while the fraternal rivalries surge, the hostility to the father abates. In her discussion of the Hebrew Bible, Regina Schwartz argues that the structure of monotheism *requires* such conflicts between brothers to deflect aggression away from the father: "Division, dissension, disparity and domination: all are paternal responses to a perceived threat of authority."[50] The descent of the French Revolution into the Terror and the ultimate advent of Napoleon perhaps speak to Freud's schema. The rise, for instance, of Stalin and Mao confirms it further. For all the hope of the age of brothers, Freud sees society condemned to repeat the Oedipal drama and return to the paternal ideal.

But Oedipus is, of course, *both* father *and* brother to his offspring. The simultaneity of these identities for Oedipus speaks to the instability at the heart of both fraternal and patriarchal societal structures.[51] And indeed, later in Freud's work he recognizes the emergence of the patriarch not so much as a given but rather as a stage of historical evolution. In *Moses and Monotheism*, his last major work, which in many ways progresses the argument of *Totem and Taboo*, Freud shows how patriarchy itself originated in the throes of a social upheaval:

> Under the influence of external conditions—which we need not follow up here and which in part are also not sufficiently known—it happened that the matriarchal structure of society was replaced by a patriarchal one. This naturally brought with it a revolution in the existing state of the law. An echo of this revolution can still be heard, I think, in the *Oresteia* of Aeschylus. This turning from the mother to the father, however, signifies above all a victory of spirituality over the

senses—that is to say a step forward in culture, since maternity is proved by the senses whereas paternity is a surmise based on a deduction and a premiss. This declaration in favour of the thought-process, thereby raising it above sense perception, has proved to be a step charged with serious consequences.[52]

Freud was not the first to see Aeschylus's *Oresteia* as an "echo" of a revolution. This reading was made popular by the Swiss jurist J. J. Bachofen in his 1861 magnum opus, *Das Mutterrecht*. Focusing on the *Eumenides*, Bachofen famously saw in the play evidence of the existence of a historical matriarchy that preceded the establishment of patriarchy.[53] Moreover, following a classically Hegelian scheme, Bachofen would ally this social development to a progression in consciousness: the move away from mothers to fathers traced a progression from materialism toward spirituality.[54] Despite his antimaterialist stance—which is still strongly felt in the Freud passage—Bachofen would have a significant impact on Friedrich Engels, who would proclaim: "The history of the family dates from 1861, from the publication of Bachofen's *Mutterrecht*."[55] In his work *Origin of the Family, Private Property, and the State* (1884), written in the immediate aftermath of Karl Marx's death (the death of another father!), Engels became preoccupied with the status of the family in the organization and distribution of capital. Although he claimed that the book was based on notes that Marx had made from his reading of Lewis H. Morgan's *Ancient Society; or, Researches in the Lines of Human Progress from Savagery, Through Barbarism to Civilization* (1877), Engels's focus on matriarchy took the Marxian analysis in a startling original direction:

> This rediscovery of the primitive matriarchal gens as the earlier stage of the patriarchal gens of civilized peoples has

the same importance for anthropology as Darwin's theory of evolution has for biology and Marx's theory of surplus value has for political economy.... The matriarchal gens has become the pivot on which the whole science turns; since its discovery we know where to look and what to look for in our research, and how to arrange the results.[56]

For Engels, Bachofen's reading of Aeschylus had become the impetus for a rethinking of the relationship between the family and the state in the era of social revolution. In the aftermath of Orestes's murder of Clytemnestra, the *Eumenides* will debate the question of the maternal bond. "And I am blood-kin to my mother?," asks Orestes.[57] It is in response to the Furies' contestation, "Do you disavow your mother's blood, the nearest and dearest to your own?," that Apollo will pass his judgment:

> The so-called "mother" is not a parent of the child, only the nurse of the newly-begotten embryo. The parent is he who mounts; the female keeps the offspring safe, like a stranger on behalf of a stranger, for those in whose case this is not prevented by god.[58]

In his introduction to *Origin of the Family*, Engels summarizes the import of Bachofen's account of the *Eumenides*:

> Bachofen interprets the *Oresteia* of Aeschylus as the dramatic representation of the conflict between declining mother-right and the new father-right that arose and triumphed in the heroic age.... [The *Eumenides* recounts that] the murder of a man not related by blood, even if he be the husband of the murderess, is expiable and does not concern the Furies; their office is solely to punish murder between blood relations, and of such murders the most grave and the

most inexpiable, according to mother-right, is matricide. Apollo now comes forward in Orestes' defense; Athena calls upon the Areopagites—the Athenian jurors—to vote; the votes for Orestes' condemnation and for his acquittal are equal; Athena, as president, gives her vote for Orestes and acquits him. Father-right has triumphed over mother-right, the "gods of young descent," as the Furies themselves call them, have triumphed over the Furies; the latter then finally allow themselves to be persuaded to take up a new office in the service of the new order.[59]

The effect of Bachofen's analysis is to figure patriarchy as the ur-revolution that brings about the new phase in civilization. While Engels endorses Bachofen's analysis of the tragedy, he nevertheless has reservations about his methods:

> This new but undoubtedly correct interpretation of the *Oresteia* is one of the best and finest passages in the whole book, but it proves at the same time that Bachofen believes at least as much as Aeschylus did in the Furies, Apollo, and Athena; for, at bottom, he believes that the overthrow of mother-right by father-right was a miracle wrought during the Greek heroic age by these divinities. That such a conception, which makes religion the lever of world history, must finally end in pure mysticism, is clear.[60]

Engels clearly parts company with Bachofen when it comes to making religion "the lever of world history." Yet he is able to map the jurist's spiritual transformation onto a materialist basis. For Engels the transition from mother-rule to father-rule tracks the development of surplus capital. As Cynthia Eller writes: "The transformation in Engels's schema occurs with the institution of the patriarchal family."[61] With the end of the rule of mothers, the patriarch enforced his power over a newly conceived nuclear family. Engels explains: "Household management lost its public character. It no longer concerned society. It became a private service; the wife became the head servant, excluded from all participation in social production."[62] The patriarchal family was tantamount to "the world historical defeat of the female sex."[63] Engels imagines its reversal under a new communist order: "With the transfer of the means of production into common ownership, the single family ceases to be the economic unit of society. Private housekeeping is transformed into a social industry. The care and education of the children becomes a public affair."[64] In *The Eighteenth Brumaire*, Marx had proclaimed: "The social revolution of the nineteenth century cannot draw its poetry from the past, but only from the future."[65] Yet, it is the *Oresteia* to which Engels turns to map out his vision of a communist (matriarchal) utopia. The reference to matriarchy may rest on fantasy rather than on a secure historical reality, but its power to structure thinking about the origins and future of the family endures.

Where Freud had seen the murder of the father as the ur-revolution, Bachofen and Engels, by contrast, see the murder of the mother as inaugurating a new age. Bachofen and Engels, then, remind Freud that before Sophocles's *Oedipus Tyrannus* came Aeschylus's *Oresteia*. Or perhaps, more correctly, these tragedies (and the revolutions they represent) occur in a constantly repeating cycle. Whereas Freud labors over the aftereffects of the death of the father in *Totem and Taboo*, he represents the advent of patriarchy as a bloodless revolution in *Moses and Monotheism*. As Hélène Cixous has it: "And one day—as Freud sees it still inscribing itself in the *Oresteia*—the matriarchy is done for, the sons stop being sons of mothers and become sons of fathers."[66] Cixous wants to reveal the suppressed violence of the Freudian interpretation:

All the energy still jammed into this end of the after-Medean afternoon (*après-Médée*), at the twilight of matriarchy, is set free once and for all. Matriarchal shrapnel scatters. The scene soaks up blood diverted from its ancient matrilinear circulation. Orestes, neuter, neither masculine nor feminine, half-active, half passive, neither criminal nor not-guilty, signs the end of the great reign of mothers. Dawn of phallocentrism.[67]

Cixous revivifies the matriarchal shrapnel that should stick in the craw of Freud's band of brothers, whose desire for the mother was, after all, the cause of their strife (as Schwartz puts it comically, "Freud only imagined one breast"![68]). Still, while the *Eumenides* announces the "dawn of phallocentrism," the middle play in Aeschylus's trilogy is located before this advent. Here instead we exist in the aftermath of the death of the father. In his account of fraternity, Jean-Luc Nancy argues that "brothers are originally orphans who have lost their father."[69] For Nancy, the political plight of democracy is the plight of these orphans. As Simon Goldhill has argued, in telling the story of (soon-to-be) orphaned siblings, Aeschylus's *Choephoroi* is intricately connected to the ideology of fifth-century Athens:

> Democracy, the constitution of Athens, restructures the commitments of the individual to the collective in a particularly heightened manner. While the household depends on hierarchy, precedence, and the authority of the *kurios* [the master], democracy privileges horizontal relationships of citizenship: equality before the law. The rhetoric of family terms shifts in a fundamental way, as the political system changes. In democracy key institutions of the family, like burial, and key terms of family affiliation are taken over by the State ("the laws are my father and mother . . ."). What is

more, brothers can become a civic, political symbol, rather than a token of family strength, as, for example, Aristogeiton and Harmodius, the brothers who killed the tyrant of Athens, were honoured in cult and drinking songs and their statues were erected in the market-place of the city.[70]

So while Oedipus may dominate the post-Freudian vision of tragedy, it is the sibling bond that so often animates the dramas of Athenian democracy. Greek tragedy speaks to an age of brotherhood (and sisterhood): Atreus and Thyestes, Orestes and Electra (and Pylades), Orestes and Iphigeneia (and Pylades), Eteocles and Polynices, Antigone and Ismene, Semele and Agave—all highlight the importance of horizontal relationships within the democratic polis.[71] The tragic dimension of these dramas (accentuated by their post–French revolutionary receptions) may confirm Freud's suspicion of the difficulty of maintaining "original democratic equality." The tragedy of fraternity can all too easily slide into the tragedy of democracy and the revival of "the ancient paternal ideal." So the French Revolution is followed by the Empire of Napoleon just as the *Choephoroi* is succeeded by the *Eumenides* with its decisive affirmation of paternity. But *pace* Freud, tragic teleology is rarely straightforward. Apollo's arguments are based on the unique example of Athena's paternity. In Euripides's later retelling in the *Orestes*, the siblings are left to their predicament against the background of a loss of all authority—both familial and political. And as Judith Butler has argued, to see *Antigone* as a prelude to the reestablishment of patriarchal norms is to fundamentally underestimate Antigone's power to undo kinship.[72] It is rather the *queerness* of familial relations that these dramas of fraternity and sorority reveal. Tragic horizontal conflicts are not a threat to democracy but rather its very essence.[73]

Carl Jung may have championed Electra as an alternative to the Oedipus complex, yet he ignored her role as a sister. In fact, the sibling bond more generally has been neglected by psychoanalysis. In her recent book, *Fratriarchy*, feminist psychoanalyst Juliet Mitchell asks us to reassess the story Freud tells in *Totem and Taboo*:

> The placing of brothers as founders of the social in *Totem and Taboo* was not developed further. So that, despite the propositions about the fraternal social contract, these lateral relations have ever since been treated as relations within the vertical family access. Brothers and sisters are simply woven as follow-ons from fathers and mothers in the Oedipal situation.[74]

But such an assimilation of sibling relations to the Oedipal, Mitchell points out, fails to recognize an important chronology:

> Most of the world today operates upon patriarchal and patrilineal vertical family lines through what has been called the "Law of the Father." When he is four or five years old, this Law is instilled in the father's son, and in his daughter in so far she is the same as her brother. This is the world-renowned but much contested "Oedipus complex." Incest with the mother is universally prohibited by the patriarch who threatens his son with castration. . . . Instead, or rather as well, I argue in this book that, prior to this stage, the mother insists on the same prohibition, but with different effects—she insists that there must be no incest or murder between her children, that is between the siblings. On the social, horizontal axis, this prohibition between siblings applies equally to sisters and her brothers, as they reach two to three years old—and it is this prohibition that I claim as the "Law of the Mother."[75]

The "Law of the Mother," the law that, in fact, founds the social, *precedes* the "Law of the Father." While Freud is quick to move on from the moment of fratriarchal social contract to refound the "Law of the Father," Mitchell asks us to linger in that moment—to sit with the "untenable" predicament of "original democratic equality" and to acknowledge the role of the mother *and* the sister in inaugurating sociality.

In David's *Oath of the Horatii* there is no mother. While the father calls the brothers to war, the absent mother recalls the missing mother of autochthony and the erasure of the many women who would take part in the French uprising. The three brothers *are* paralleled by three women who may be wives *or* sisters, but this identification has no consequence, for they are at the margins of the image and the event (that one of these brothers will later kill one of these women is set up not to matter). But, with Mitchell in mind, we could reread the scene. If the central figure of the father is removed, what we have is two groups of three. Perhaps rather than a father handing (phallic) swords to his sons, we have a depiction of two competing stories of origin: matriarchy versus patriarchy, the *Oresteia* versus *Oedipus*. If we squint, could we see a sword suspended between Orestes and Clytemnestra rather than Oedipus and Laius? The most distant of the three women may not be *the* mother, but she certainly appears to be *a* mother. She shields two siblings (?) of indeterminate gender in her cloak, and while she offers them affection might she also be quietly enforcing the "Law of the Mother"?

Epilogue

In the introduction we discussed Hannah Arendt's observation that "revolutions, properly speaking, did not exist prior to the modern age."[1] Modern uprisings, as we have been examining, have repeatedly drawn their inspiration from ancient ideals, but revolution, as such, has no ancient precedent. Revolutions are part of what make modernity modernity. In 1963, Arendt confidently asserted that "whatever the outcome of our present predicaments may be, if we don't perish altogether, it seems more than likely that revolution... will stay with us for the foreseeable future."[2] Arendt's belief in the resilience of revolution as a mode of political action is as striking as her caveat about the possibility of total annihilation. The existential threat that Arendt alludes to is presumably nuclear war. Yet as Slavoj Žižek argues in *First as Tragedy, Then as Farce*, written in the immediate aftermath of the 2008 financial crisis, faith in revolution has not matched Arendt's expectations. While billions of dollars were speedily invested in a crashing global banking system, no comparable effort has been made to halt environmental devastation. In 2008, as global capitalism flailed, mass uprising was averted. If the "physiognomy" of the twentieth century was unimaginable to Arendt without revolution, a prime characteristic of the twenty-first century so far has been the missing revolution.[3]

Events such as the Arab Spring that followed closely on the back of the 2008 crash might suggest that such a perspective ignores the global south. But as the Arab Spring was met with authoritarian repression and the reconsolidation of power, it turned into a long Arab Winter.[4] Perhaps we are back to the *metabolai* of antiquity? As Hobbes phrases it at the end of *Behemoth*: "I have seen in this revolution a circular motion of the sovereign power."[5] Popular movements continue to emerge in the Arab world as elsewhere, but we are left today more with a sense of permacrisis than with hope for the "emancipation of all mankind through revolution" envisioned by Arendt. In Europe and the Americas, while popular protests around LBGTQ+ rights and racial injustice have been transformative, revolution is imagined simultaneously as a danger to freedom and its expression. Moreover, where revolution may seem to be in the offing and is certainly invoked by name, it is in the context of the specter of January 6 and the rise of authoritarian populism. Here revolution is pitted against democracy.

How are we to narrate this new situation of *stasis*? Žižek holds on to the classical/Hegelian/Marxian trope "first as tragedy, then as farce" while reminding us that "Herbert Marcuse added yet another turn of the screw: sometimes, the repetition in the form of farce can be more terrifying than the original tragedy."[6] Whereas Arendt envisioned a rectilinear movement of time propelled by the political revolutions of the eighteenth and nineteenth centuries, we seem to have reverted or revolved back to a more ancient conception, in which faith in the new is tempered by a recognition of the inevitability of return. The past, as we have explored in this book, persists in even the most forward-looking moments of revolutionary change. The attachment to the past can be reactionary in character, envisioning an idealized antiquity that preexisted the corruptions of modernity. One can think of many such examples of the reception of Greece and Rome, from neofascism in Italy to Trump's Spartan warriors marching on the Capitol. But it can also have the form of Benjamin's *Jetztzeit*, acting as a force that detaches us from the continuum of history, which precisely disrupts the linear movement of time on a predictable axis. David's painting *The Lictors Bring to Brutus the Bodies of His Sons*, commissioned by the king before the start of the French Revolution but displayed in its initial throes, speaks to these paradoxes in time. In informing the depiction of the aftermath of a tyrannicide, antiquity here is functioning as much as a prediction as a backward gaze. But the painting is untimely in a different sense: even at the moment of its rapturous reception by the revolutionaries, this work of art suggests the costs as much as the ecstasies of emancipation. The painting appears to depict Brutus's steadfast devotion to the new republic as tragedy for the family who surround him. In anticipation of Hegel's post–French revolutionary reading of *Antigone* that anatomizes the predicament of women in the *polis*, an alternative title for David's painting could be "the eternal irony of the community."[7]

Here we see how the forms of classicism—tragedy, Roman historiography, republican ideals—can give meaning and shape to the flux of history both during and after events. Revolutionaries such as Marx were suspicious of these formal trappings even as they perpetuated them in their own analyses of revolution. The grand classical genres of the old revolutions were supposed to give way to a new authentic expression of the popular will beyond all forms of representation—political and aesthetic. Classical forms may again appear inadequate in capturing the accelerated pace of political change today. Generic categories such as tragedy can bestow disingenuous meaning and legibility onto senseless suffering and devastation. Formal coherence may have worn itself out in the relentless waves of new crises. Yet, the search for agency beyond representation seems ever more deluded in an age when posting on social media has become the most popular mode of direct action. "The only way to grasp the true novelty of the New," Žižek writes, "is to analyze the world through the lenses of what was 'eternal' in the Old. If communism really is an 'eternal' Idea... it is eternal not in the sense of a series of abstract-universal features that may be applied everywhere, but in the sense that it has to be reinvented in each new historical situation."[8] If all invention is reinvention, then antiquity is just such an "eternal"—that is, it is remade for each epoch, and it is these remakes of the old that point to the truly new. The tragedies of the twenty-first century will not be the tragedies of the nineteenth century, just as those tragedies differed substantially from the tragedies of the fifth century BCE. Tragedy's potential to convey the paradoxes of agency, the hopes and deceptions of emancipation, or the ironies of revolution does not yet appear to have been exhausted.

Perhaps the modernity of revolution, then, lies not in revolution itself but in the compulsion to recount political change in a tragic key. Invoking the stories of Cain and Abel and Romulus and Remus, Arendt writes: "Whatever brotherhood human beings may be capable of has grown out of fratricide, whatever political organization men may have achieved has its origins in crime."[9] Fraternity, here, is not conceived of as a utopian ideal so much as a solution to the problem of tragic violence, a way to staunch the blood. Just as in the *Oresteia* the institutions of democracy are presented as the compromise men make with the bloodshed of the past, so modern revolutions carry the violence of their origins into their destructive execution. If, since the French Revolution, *fraternity* has become the byword of liberal democracy, its origins in manifold feuds of ancient brothers (and sisters) remind us that contestation, conflict, and plurality are—and have to be—ineliminable parts of democratic politics. Ancient brothers and the broader classical ideology of fraternity are also a reminder of the violence of fratriarchy and its gendered and racial assumptions.

This book has looked at the themes of time, genre, and fraternity to understand the continuing impact of Greece and Rome on modern political revolt. It explored how revolutions put pressure on chronology, exposing the new as old and the old as new. It showed how both the actors and commentators on revolution drew on ancient drama to make sense of the performance of political action, its triumphs and its failures. It examined the classical references that underpin the revolutionary proclamation of universal brotherhood, revealing both the limits of its universalism and the conflicts it evades.

If, as Arendt suggests, revolutions are coextensive with modernity, then we can see today that even as conventional revolutions wilt, modernity persists. "Modernity" is, as it were, too big to fail. Yet, thanks to its perceived lack of foundations, the classics are brought in to prop up what might otherwise founder. As we saw with the example of the Republican calendar, in the secular age, the Greco-Roman past can become a placeholder for discredited theological structures. Like the Judeo-Christian God it displaced, might antiquity itself one day be killed off? Marx argued that the "tradition of all the dead generations weighs like a nightmare on the brain of the living."[10] Perhaps it is in its status as always already dead that antiquity's power resides. The specter of a zombie classics continues to haunt modernity. The *classical* and the *revolutionary* might appear to be antonyms. By drawing out the classicism of revolution, this book has shown how the reference to the past in political action endures and enables even as it constrains.

Acknowledgments

This is a small book on a big topic. I am very grateful to Brooke Holmes and Mark Payne, the editors of the Critical Antiquities series, for encouraging me in this act of hubris. Brooke has been a cherished interlocutor throughout the project and I'm grateful to her for her invaluable advice and intellectual example. At the University of Chicago Press, I'm indebted to Susan Bielstein, Karen Levine, and Victoria Barry, who made the process of publication so smooth, to my excellent copy editor, Stephen Twilley, and to the anonymous readers of the manuscript, for their many perceptive comments and helpful suggestions.

The initial idea for this project took shape after I was invited to give the Roberts Lectures at Dickinson College—many thanks indeed to my generous hosts on that occasion, especially to Marc Mastrangelo. I have subsequently been fortunate to present this work at conferences and seminars at a number of different institutions: Berkeley, Cambridge, Dundee, Manchester, Oxford, Princeton, Thessaloniki, and Utrecht. Heartfelt thanks to the audiences and, in particular, to Carol Atack, Joshua Billings, Mauricio Bonazzi, Ekin Bodur, Richard Bourke, Chris Brooke, Clare Foster, Jeremy Glick, Jessica Glueck, Emma Greensmith, Constanze Güthenke, John Hamilton, Ramona Naddaff, Peter Porman, Jim Porter, Tim Rood, Frank Ruda, Evanthia Sistakou, Mario Telò, Alberto Toscano, Mathura Umachandran, and Tim Whitmarsh. It was a particular honor to have the opportunity to engage again with Srinivas

Aravamudan's ideas. Thanks are also due to Katherine Harloe, Adam Lecznar, Helen Morales, Sanja Perovic, and Victoria Wohl, for many pivotal conversations and suggestions. I have learned a great deal from their work.

I am grateful to my University College London colleagues Stephen Colvin, Fiachra Mac Góráin, Gesine Manuwald, and Maria Wyke, and to the broader London classics community. I also thank my PhD students Angelica Baker-Ottoway, Melina Lourou, Faye Mather, Alex Meghji, Mélissa Pires Da Silva, Ben Temblett, Chloe Tye, and Tom Willis, as well as the students in my Athens in Modern Political Theory module, for their lively debates and contributions to many of the topics discussed in this book.

Aude Doody, Katie Fleming, and Annelise Freisenbruch provided succor and tea both literal and conceptual over many years of peerless friendship.

Simon Goldhill, Daniel Orrells, and Phiroze Vasunia read several versions of the manuscript and responded with characteristic brilliance—I am extremely fortunate to have such an extraordinary coterie. Bonnie Honig was my first and last reader and shaped the project in innumerable ways; it is a rare blessing to have such an incisive interlocutor and treasured friend.

Finally, my unending love and gratitude to my family: to Mark, Gabs, Jakob, and Noa; to my mother, Irène, who provided inspiration and precious support both intellectual and practical, and to my father, Dick, who taught me about politics, and whom I miss so much; to Phiroze, whose daily encouragement and love makes everything possible. This book is dedicated to our darling Isaac, who staged a revolution in our lives and liberated us from the ancien régime.

Notes

INTRODUCTION

1 On the history of the term, see Williams, *Keywords*, 270–74.
2 Among a huge bibliography, see Ober, *Athenian Revolution*; Syme, *Roman Revolution*; and Goldhill and Osborne, *Rethinking Revolutions Through Ancient Greece*. For a recent account of political resistance under the Roman Empire, see Jolowicz and Elsner, *Articulating Resistance Under the Roman Empire*.
3 For a more nuanced account of the ancient attitude to change, see D'Angour, *Greeks and the New*, and, specifically on revolution, Whitmarsh, "(Not) Talkin' 'bout a Revolution."
4 Shapin, *Scientific Revolution*, 3.
5 Arendt, *On Revolution*, 2.
6 Garcia, *Life Intense*, 6–7.
7 Kant, *Political Writings*, 54.
8 Quoted in Goldfarb, *Emancipation*, 58.
9 See Altmann, *Moses Mendelssohn*, 148–49.
10 *Writings and Speeches of Edmund Burke*, 8:314.
11 Mainz, "Bringing the Hemlock Up," masterfully tells the complex story of the painting's reception through print in the revolutionary period.
12 Wilson, *Death of Socrates*, 177.
13 Winckelmann, *History of the Art of Antiquity*, 299.
14 Winkelmann, *Geschichte der Kunst der Alterthums*, 234, as translated in Potts, *Flesh and the Ideal*, 54.
15 *Collected Works of Mahatma Gandhi*, 8:246–47; on which, see Vasunia, "Gandhi and Socrates."
16 *Collected Works of Mahatma Gandhi*, 8:248.
17 *Collected Works of Mahatma Gandhi*, 8:247.
18 *Collected Works of Mahatma Gandhi*, 8:247.

19 Fanon, *Wretched of the Earth*, 27.
20 Fanon, 28.
21 Fanon, 27.
22 King, *Why We Can't Wait*, 80–81.
23 King, 79–80.
24 Furet, *Interpreting the French Revolution*, 3.
25 Arendt, *On Revolution*, 51.
26 See Bayly, *Birth of the Modern World*; Sivasundaram, *Waves Across the South*; and Armitage and Subrahmanyam, *Age of Revolutions in Global Context*.
27 Koselleck, *Vergangene Zukunft*, 68–69 (my translation).
28 Marx, *Eighteenth Brumaire*, 10.
29 Goldhill, "Resisting Resistance," 240.
30 Marx, *Eighteenth Brumaire*, 11.

TIME

1 See Rood et al., *Anachronism and Antiquity*, for fascinating discussions of ancient chronology and its reception.
2 Comay, *Mourning Sickness*, 7.
3 Arendt, *On Revolution*, 1.
4 Arendt, 2.
5 Arendt, 19.
6 See Perovic, *Calendar in Revolutionary France*.
7 Perovic, 1.
8 For this shift in the understanding of time, see Goldhill, *Christian Invention of Time*.
9 See the exhibition catalogue for *Glorious Years: French Calendars from Louis XIV to the Revolution*, curated by Rachel Jacobs, Waddesdon Manor, Aylesbury, Buckinghamshire, March 22–October 28, 2018, accessed January 7, 2024, available at https://waddesdon.org.uk/whats-on/glorious-years-exhibition/.
10 Taylor, *Secular Age*, 208.
11 Perovic, *Calendar in Revolutionary France*, 11.
12 Schmitt, *Political Theology*, 36.
13 Arendt, *Between Past and Future*, 43–44 and 278n5, trans. Denver Lindley.
14 Arendt, 44.

15 Augustine, *City of God* 12.20.
16 Momigliano, "Time in Ancient Historiography"; see also Whitmarsh, "(Not) Talkin' 'bout a Revolution."
17 Möller and Luraghi, "Time in the Writing of History," 7.
18 Perovic, *Calendar in Revolutionary France*, 7.
19 Comay, *Mourning Sickness*, 7.
20 On the Revolution as drama, see Comay, *Mourning Sickness*.
21 For Arendt on tragedy, see Pirro, *Hannah Arendt and the Politics of Tragedy*, and Leonard, *Tragic Modernities*.
22 Arendt, *On Revolution*, 24.
23 Arendt, 24.
24 Arendt, 11.
25 Plato, *Republic* 8, 546a.
26 For a different typology of Greek revolutionary consciousness, see Whitmarsh, "(Not) Talkin' 'bout a Revolution."
27 In *On Revolution*, Arendt discusses the etymology of the word at 25–26 and 32–34.
28 Koselleck, *Practice of Conceptual History*, 152.
29 Koselleck, *Futures Past*, 49.
30 Koselleck, 53.
31 Marx, *Eighteenth Brumaire*, 10.
32 Derrida quoted in Kearney, *Debates in Continental Philosophy*, 112.
33 Marx, *Eighteenth Brumaire*, 11.
34 Benjamin, *Illuminations*, 263.
35 Marx, *Eighteenth Brumaire*, 11; see also Cowley and Martin, *Marx's "Eighteenth Brumaire"*, 5.
36 Derrida, *Specters of Marx*, 110 (Derrida's emphasis).
37 Arendt, *On Revolution*, 111–12.
38 The painting originated as an engraving in 1790, and David attempted to raise funds for a full-scale painting. The painting was revised by David and his followers over a number of years.
39 Marx, *Eighteenth Brumaire*, 10.
40 Marx, *Eighteenth Brumaire*, 12–13.
41 Arendt, *On Revolution*, 25.
42 Chateaubriand, *Essai sur les révolutions*, 90 (my translation).
43 Chateaubriand, preface to *Essai sur les révolutions*, quoted in Hartog, *Anciens, Modernes, Sauvages*, 55 (my translation).

44 Volney, *Leçons d'histoire*, 140 (my translation).
45 Hartog, *Anciens, modernes, sauvages*, 69.
46 Quoted in Hartog, 59 (my translation).
47 Winckelmann, *Geschichte der Kunst des Alterthums*, 3 (my translation).
48 See Potts, *Flesh and the Ideal*, and Hartog, *Anciens, modernes, sauvages*.
49 Ferris, *Silent Urns*, 33.
50 Delécluze, *Louis David*, 71–72 (my translation).
51 Ozouf, "Fraternity," 817.
52 Marx, *Eighteenth Brumaire*, 10.

GENRE

"The Revolution Will Not Be Televised": Gil Scott-Heron. Epigraph: Nietzsche, *Beyond Good and Evil*, trans. Helen Zimmern.

1 Comay, *Mourning Sickness*, 26.
2 Comay, 26.
3 Comay, 50.
4 Kant, *Conflict of the Faculties*, 153.
5 Heine, *On the History of Religion and Philosophy*, 115.
6 Schlegel, "Athenaeum Fragments," 118 (translation slightly modified), discussed in Comay, *Mourning Sickness*, 24.
7 Comay, *Mourning Sickness*, 24.
8 Schlegel is, of course, writing against the background of the birth of *Altertumswissenschaft*. Wolf's foundational *Prolegomena ad Homerum* was published in 1795. On this background, see Harloe, *Winckelmann and the Invention of Antiquity*, and Güthenke, *Feeling and Classical Philology*.
9 Marx, *Early Writings*, 49.
10 Marx and Engels, *Collected Works*, 19:245.
11 Marx and Engels, 247–48, quoted and discussed in Žižek, *First as Tragedy*, 2. On this passage, see also Prawer, *Marx and World Literature*, 64–65.
12 Marx, *Eighteenth Brumaire*, 10.
13 See Mazlish, "Tragic Farce of Marx, Hegel, and Engels."
14 See Paolucci and Paolucci, *Hegel on Tragedy*.

15 Mazlish outlines Marx's ultimate debt to Engels in the use of comedy and tragedy as historical tropes.
16 Marx, *Eighteenth Brumaire*, 11.
17 Marx, 11–12.
18 Marx and Engels, *Collected Works*, 19:250.
19 Such an assessment of Lincoln is strongly contested by Wills, *Lincoln at Gettysburg*, which offers a forensic analysis of the classical parallels in the Gettysburg Address.
20 Marx and Engels, *Collected Works*, 19:250–21.
21 Brooks, *Melodramatic Imagination*.
22 Stallybrass, "'Well Grubbed, Old Mole,'" 6.
23 Marx, *Eighteenth Brumaire*, 10.
24 Nietzsche, *Untimely Meditations*, 59.
25 See Arasse, *La Guillotine*, and Gerould, *Guillotine*.
26 Burke, *Revolutionary Writings*, 73. "Old Jewry" refers to a district in the City of London that had been the Jewish Ghetto before the expulsion of the Jews in 1290. It was the location of a well-known Nonconformist meeting house where Richard Price preached. Price is frequently targeted by Burke in the *Reflections*. See the notes to Burke, lii–liii.
27 Burke, 77.
28 Deane, *Foreign Affections*, 64.
29 Quoted in Comay, *Mourning Sickness*, 51.
30 Comay, 51.
31 Comay, 51.
32 Quoted in Comay, 51–52.
33 Comay, 52.
34 Deane, *Foreign Affections*, 90.
35 Marx, *Eighteenth Brumaire*, 12–13.
36 Derrida, *Specters of Marx*, 142.
37 Derrida, 144.
38 I borrow this term from Aravamudan, *Tropicopolitans*.
39 Buck-Morss, "Hegel and Haiti," 821.
40 So George Armstrong Kelly: "In the background always and at the surface much of the time Hegel is wrestling with problems of Greek antiquity and seeking both to overcome them and to externalize them in an alien climate. The Platonic parallel between struggles in the state and struggles in the soul is never far dis-

tant. I will permit myself the liberty of saying that the great figures of Aristotle, Plato, and Sophocles bestride, respectively, the sections on *Bewusstsein, Selbstbewusstsein*, and *Geist*." "Notes on Hegel's 'Lordship and Bondage,'" 260.

41 Shklar, "Self-Sufficient Man," 291–92.
42 Marx and Engels, *Collected Works*, 19:79.
43 Buck-Morss, *Hegel, Haiti, and Universal History*, 56.
44 Buck-Morss, 48.
45 Arthur, "Hegel and the French Revolution," 18.
46 See Comay, *Mourning Sickness*; Arthur, "Hegel and the French Revolution"; Ritter, *Hegel and the French Revolution*; and, for a magisterial account of Hegel's relationship to the concept of revolution itself, Bourke, *Hegel's World Revolution*.
47 Buck-Morss, "Hegel and Haiti," 836.
48 Rousseau, *The Social Contract*, 41.
49 Buck Morss, "Hegel and Haiti," 830.
50 See Sala-Molins, *Le Code Noir*.
51 Quoted in James, *Black Jacobins*, 23.
52 James, *Black Jacobins*, 24.
53 Aravamudan, "Trop(Icaliz)ing the Enlightenment," 55.
54 Quoted in James, *Black Jacobins*, 60.
55 Buck-Morss, *Hegel, Haiti, and Universal History*, 41.
56 Aravamudan, *Tropicopolitans*, 308.
57 The membership of the Amis des Noirs was made up principally of Girondins. It was the Girondins who kept the issue of slavery in public view during the early years of the revolution. They initially advocated the abolition of the slave trade rather than slavery itself. When the National Assembly finally voted to abolish slavery, in 1794, the Girondins had been proscribed and the Amis des Noirs had ceased to meet.
58 The ten-volume tome underwent many revisions, notably in a third edition, published in 1780, which was significantly reworked by Denis Diderot.
59 Quoted in James, *Black Jacobins*, 25. On the apocryphal nature of this scene, see Aravamudan, *Tropicopolitans*, 303.
60 James, *Black Jacobins*, 25.
61 Aravamudan, *Tropicopolitans*, 302.
62 Of the seven explicit references to tragedy in *The Black Jacobins*,

five make reference to the tensions between heroes and masses. In particular, Robespierre's relationship to the Parisian workers is depicted as a tragic one (177).
63 Scott, *Conscripts of Modernity*, 36.
64 White, *Metahistory*, 8–9.
65 White, 9.
66 See Rabbitt, "C. L. R. James's Figuring of Toussaint-Louverture."
67 This is the standard reading of Toussaint's nom de guerre. A more prosaic account suggests it was connected to his gapped teeth. See Aravamudan, *Tropicopolitans*, 324.
68 See James, *Notes on Dialectics*.
69 See Glick, *Black Radical Tragic*; McConnell, "Staging the Haitian Revolution in London"; and Douglas, *Making the Black Jacobins*.
70 See Langerwerf, "Universal Slave Revolts."
71 James, *American Civilization*, 153–54.
72 Glick, *Black Radical Tragic*, 139.
73 James, *Black Jacobins*, 26.
74 James, x.
75 Aravamudan's *Tropicopolitans* shows how the Haitian context upends Marx's narrative about historical sequence: "Dessalines, the first leader of independent Haiti, preceded Napoleon in declaring himself an emperor; Soulouque declared himself Emperor Faustin I of Haiti in 1849, before Louis Napoleon did the equivalent in France in 1851. The Parisian press dubbed the nephew's monarchical extravagance Soulouquerie, resulting in a French decree banning the use of the term. We may modify Marx's assertion that historical repetition shows the degeneration of tragedy into farce. Farce and tragedy are coimplicated with each other at the colonialist origin, reminding us of another black Spartacus, Oroonoko" (314–15). Moreover, James in his characterization of San Domingo as a protocapitalist society will further see the Haitian Revolution as a more successful precursor to the communist revolution of 1917.
76 James, *Black Jacobins*, 289–90. These paragraphs were inserted by James into the 1963 edition of the final chapter on "The War of Independence." On which, see Scott, *Conscripts of Modernity*.
77 Scott, *Conscripts of Modernity*, 163.

78 Scott, 163–64.
79 In fact, James sets up the comparison between Toussaint and Prometheus to ultimately differentiate between them, claiming that Toussaint's tragedy was of a "lesser category." *Black Jacobins*, 291.
80 Arendt, *On Revolution*, 273.
81 Quoted in Aravamudan, *Tropicopolitans*, 316.
82 Aravamudan, 317.
83 Ovid, *Metamorphoses* VII, 257–63.
84 Ovid, 285–95.
85 The Diderot-Raynal passage is probably in dialogue with Hobbes's earlier reading of the Pelias episode. The episode is also taken up by Burke in his *Reflections*. See Aravamudan, *Tropicopolitans*, 318.
86 Aravamudan, *Tropicopolitans*, 317.
87 Aravamudan, 323.
88 James, *Black Jacobins*, ix.
89 From a 1969 interview with Césaire, in *Écrits politiques*, 291. On Césaire, the Haitian Revolution, and classicism, see Lecznar, "Tragedy of Aimé Césaire."
90 White, *Metahistory*, 9.
91 Du Bois, *Black Reconstruction*, 727.
92 Toscano, "Tragedy and Jubilee," 354–55, quoting Roediger, "Accounting for the Wages of Whiteness," 23.
93 Marx, *Eighteenth Brumaire*, 10.
94 Nietzsche, *Beyond Good and Evil*, 11, taken up by Simon Critchley in *Tragedy, the Greeks, and US* in his discussion of tragedy.
95 Toscano, "Oneself as an Enemy," 260.

FRATERNITY

1 Quoted in Ozouf, "Fraternity," 702.
2 See Oakley, "Dionysius of Halicarnassus and Livy."
3 On the relationship of David to Corneille, see Gutwirth, *Corneille's "Horace" and David's "Oath of the Horatii"*.
4 See Michel and Sahut, *David*.
5 Schama, *Power of Art*, 196.
6 Crow, "The *Oath of the Horatii* in 1785."

7   See Boime, *Art in an Age of Revolution*, 393.
8   Schama, *Power of Art*, 196.
9   As Schama, in his review of *A Palace for a King*, by Jonathan Brown and J. H. Elliott, acerbically notes: "This is the sort of thing that gives the historical-art historical collaboration a bad name" (684).
10 Ozouf, "Fraternity," 694.
11 Ozouf, 694.
12 See also Paul's Letter to the Romans 8: 14–16.
13 See Puyol, *Political Fraternity*, for a discussion of Joseph Ratzinger's distinction between the "universalist interpretation of Christian fraternity ... [and] the unmistakable universality of the Enlightened fraternity, which would not appear until the French Revolution" (14).
14 Plato, *Republic* III, 415a.
15 Plato, *Menexenus*, 238e–239a.
16 See especially Loraux, *Divided City*.
17 Plato, *Menexenus* 238a.
18 Plato, 237 b-c.
19 Derrida, *Politics of Friendship*, viii.
20 Derrida, viii.
21 Derrida, viii.
22 See Lambert, *Phratries of Attica*.
23 Derrida, *Politics of Friendship*, 92.
24 For a history of divergent readings of the *Menexenus* and its tone, see Clavaud, *Ménexène de Platon*.
25 Derrida, *Politics of Friendship*, 92–93.
26 It is an irony for both Derrida and his comments about democracy and the European Union that it is now the far right that seems to have a monopoly on the vocabulary of brotherhood (e.g., Giorgia Meloni's Brothers of Italy party).
27 "European Anthem," European Union, accessed October 30, 2024, https://european-union.europa.eu/principles-countries-history/symbols/european-anthem_en.
28 Engelstein, *Sibling Action*, 61.
29 Engelstein, 62.
30 Nancy, "Fraternity," 121.
31 Schwartz, *Curse of Cain*, 109.

32 Nancy, "Fraternity," 121.
33 Derrida, *Politics of Friendship*, viii–ix (emphasis in original). The risk may be that "sorority" merely becomes an additive. Nevertheless Bonnie Honig, in *Antigone Interrupted*, has shown that the resistance to understanding Antigone and Ismene as collaborators reveals sorority's potential to disturb the old order (151–89). As she later clarified: "Sorority doesn't stand for sisters as such but for the unimaginable that fraternity disappears from view" (private correspondence).
34 See the famous wish expressed by Goethe: "I would give a great deal for an apt philologist to prove that it is interpolated and spurious" (Eckermann, *Conversations of Goethe with Eckermann and Soret*, 177).
35 Sophocles, *Antigone* 905–13.
36 Edelman, *No Future*; on which, see also Honig, *Antigone Interrupted*.
37 Hunt, *Family Romance*, xiv.
38 Aristotle, *Politics*, 1160b. For a fascinating study of paternal authority, see Weineck, *Tragedy of Fatherhood*.
39 Hunt, *Family Romance*, 53.
40 *Journal de la République française* (one of the many variations on *L'ami du peuple*), January 12, 1793; quoted in Hunt, *Family Romance*, 57.
41 Hunt, *Family Romance*, 59.
42 Freud, *Standard Edition*, 13:141–42.
43 Freud, 13:143.
44 Balzac, *Mémoires de deux jeunes mariées*, 75, as translated by R. S. Scott.
45 See Hunt, *Family Romance*, 64–68.
46 Honig, *Feminist Theory of Refusal*.
47 Weineck, "Laius Syndrome," 137.
48 Hunt, *Family Romance*, 72.
49 Freud, *Standard Edition*, 13:148–49.
50 Schwartz, *Curse of Cain*, 109. Schwartz argues that the *Greek* mythological basis of Freud's complex is no accident: "What is noteworthy about [the Oedipus complex] is that Freud had to turn to a Greek myth to find it. The Hebrew Bible wouldn't yield the narrative of slaying the father" (110).

51 My thanks to Mario Telò for this important insight.
52 Freud, *Standard Edition*, 23:113–14.
53 Froma Zeitlin, in her seminal article on matriarchal myths in the *Oresteia*, writes: "Matriarchy in the literal meaning of the term is not provable as a historical reality. Far more compelling is Bamberger's theory of the myth of matriarchy as myth, 'not a memory of history, but a social charter,' which 'may be part of social history in providing justification for a present and perhaps permanent reality by giving an invented 'historical' explanation of how this reality is created" ("Dynamics of Misogyny," 151).
54 Bachofen, *Mutterrecht*; see also Eller, *Gentlemen and Amazons*, 42–43.
55 Engels, *Origin of the Family*, 39.
56 Engels, *Origin of the Family*, 48. On the background to Engels's book, see Eller, *Gentlemen and Amazons*.
57 Aeschylus, *Eumenides* 606.
58 Aeschylus, *Eumenides* 607–8, 657–61.
59 Engels, *Origin of the Family*, 40–41.
60 Engels, 41.
61 Eller, *Gentlemen and Amazons*, 112.
62 For a parallel explanation of the effects of "scarcity" on family dynamics in the Hebrew Bible, see Schwartz, *Curse of Cain*, xi.
63 Engels, *Origin of the Family*, 87,
64 Engels, 139.
65 Marx, *Eighteenth Brumaire*, 12–13.
66 Cixous, "Sorties," 103.
67 Cixous, 105.
68 Schwartz, *Curse of Cain*, 116.
69 Nancy, "Fraternity," 122.
70 Goldhill, "Antigone and the Politics of Sisterhood," 148.
71 See especially Honig, *Antigone Interrupted* and *A Feminist Theory of Refusal*.
72 Butler, *Antigone's Claim*. Butler interestingly does not adopt the language of sisterhood, opting instead for the broader concept of kinship; see also Freeman, *Queer Kinship*.
73 See Honig, *Antigone Interrupted* and *A Feminist Theory of Refusal*, for democracy as a site of (tragic) agonistic sorority.

74 Mitchell, *Fratriarchy*, 73.
75 Mitchell, 4.

EPILOGUE

1 Arendt, *On Revolution*, 2.
2 Arendt, 2.
3 For this term and wider insightful analysis, see Butler, "A Circular Motion."
4 The term was first employed by Chinese political scientist Zhang Weiwei, debating the possibility of the spread of revolution with Francis Fukuyama.
5 Hobbes, *Behemoth*, 204.
6 Žižek, *First as Tragedy*, 5.
7 Hegel, *Phenomenology of Spirit*, 288.
8 Žižek, *First as Tragedy*, 6.
9 Arendt, *On Revolution*, 10.
10 Marx, *Eighteenth Brumaire*, 10.

Works Cited

Aeschylus, *Eumenides*. Translated by Alan H. Sommerstein. Harvard University Press, 2009.

Altmann, Alexander. *Moses Mendelssohn: A Biographical Study*. London, 1973.

Arasse, Daniel. *La Guillotine et l'imaginaire de la Terreur*. Flammarion, 1987.

Aravamudan, Srinivas. "Trop(Icaliz)ing the Enlightenment." In "Histoires Coloniales," edited by Elizabeth Ezra, special issue, *Diacritics* 23, no. 3, (1993): 48–68.

Aravamudan, Srinivas. *Tropicopolitans: Colonialism and Agency, 1688–1804*. Duke University Press, 1999.

Arendt, Hannah. *Between Past and Future: Eight Exercises in Political Thought*. Penguin, 2006

Arendt, Hannah. *On Revolution*. Penguin, 2006.

Aristotle, *Politics*. Translated by H. Rackham. Harvard University Press, 2014.

Armitage, David, and Sanjay Subrahmanyam, eds. *The Age of Revolutions in Global Context, c. 1760–1840*. Palgrave Macmillan, 2010.

Arthur, Chris. "Hegel and the French Revolution." *Radical Philosophy* 52 (1989): 18–21.

Augustine, *City of God*. Translated by George E. McCracken. Loeb Classical Library 411. Harvard University Press, 1957.

Bachofen, J. J. *Mutterrecht: A Study of Religious and Juridical Aspects of Gynecocracy in the Ancient World*. Translated and abridged by David Partenheimer. Edwin Mellen Press, 2007.

Balzac. *Letters of Two Brides*. Translated by R. S. Scott. London, 1897.

Bayly, C. A. *The Birth of the Modern World, 1780–1914: Global Connections and Comparisons*. Blackwell, 2004.
Beiser, Frederick C., ed. *The Early Political Writings of the German Romantics*. Translated by Frederick C. Beiser. Cambridge University Press, 1996.
Benjamin, Walter. *Illuminations*. Edited by Hannah Arendt. Translated by Harry Zohn. Fontana, 1973.
Boime, Albert. *Art in an Age of Revolution, 1750–1800*. University of Chicago Press, 1987.
Bourke, Richard. *Hegel's World Revolutions*. Princeton University Press, 2023.
Brooks, Peter. *The Melodramatic Imagination: Balzac, Henry James, Melodrama, and the Mode of Excess*. Yale University Press, 1976.
Buck-Morss, Susan. "Hegel and Haiti." *Critical Inquiry* 26, no. 4 (2000): 821–65.
Buck-Morss, Susan. *Hegel, Haiti, and Universal History*. University of Pittsburgh Press, 2009.
Burke, Edmund. *Revolutionary Writings*. Edited by Iain Hampsher-Monk. Cambridge University Press, 2014.
Burke, Edmund. *The Writings and Speeches of Edmund Burke*, edited by Paul Langford. Vol 8, *The French Revolution, 1790–1794*, edited by L. G. Mitchell and William B. Todd. Clarendon Press, 1989.
Butler, James. "A Circular Motion: Protest, What Is It Good For?" *London Review of Books*, February 8, 2024.
Butler, Judith. *Antigone's Claim: Kinship Between Life and Death*. Columbia University Press, 2002.
Césaire, Aimé. *Écrits politiques: 1957–1971*. Jean-Michel Place, 2016.
Chateaubriand, Francois-René de. *Essai sur les révolutions—Génie du Christianisme*. Edited by Maurice Regard. Gallimard, 1978.
Cixous, Hélène. "Sorties: Out and Out: Attacks / Ways Out / Forays." In Hélène Cixous and Catherine Clément, *The Newly Born Woman*. Translated by Betsy Wing. I. B. Tauris, 1996.
Clavaud, Robert. *Le Ménexène de Platon et la rhétorique de son temps*. Belles Lettres, 1987.
Comay, Rebecca. *Mourning Sickness: Hegel and the French Revolution*. Stanford University Press, 2011.

Cowley, Mark, and James Martin, eds. *Marx's "Eighteenth Brumaire": (Post)Modern Interpretations*. Pluto Press, 2002.
Critchley, Simon. *Tragedy, the Greeks, and Us*. Profile, 2019.
Crow, Thomas. "The *Oath of the Horatii* in 1785: Painting and Pre-Revolutionary Radicalism in France." *Art History* 1, no. 4 (1978): 424–71.
D'Angour, Armand. *The Greeks and the New: Novelty in Ancient Greek Imagination and Experience*. Cambridge University Press, 2011.
Deane, Seamus. *Foreign Affections: Essays on Edmund Burke*. Cork University Press, 2005.
Delécluze, M. E. J. *Louis David: Son école et son temps*. Paris, 1855.
Derrida, Jacques. *The Politics of Friendship*. Translated by George Collins. Verso, 1997.
Derrida, Jacques. *Specters of Marx: The State of the Debt, the Work of Mourning, and the New International*. Translated by Peggy Kamuf. Routledge, 1994.
Douglas, Rachel. *Making the Black Jacobins: C. L. R James and the Drama of History*. Duke University Press, 2019.
Du Bois, W. E. B. *Black Reconstruction in America, 1860–1880*. Free Press, 1998.
Eckermann, Johann Peter. *Conversations of Goethe with Eckermann and Soret*. Translated by John Oxenford. Cambridge University Press, 2011.
Edelman, Lee. *No Future: Queer Theory and the Death Drive*. Duke University Press, 2004.
Eller, Cynthia. *Gentlemen and Amazons: The Myth of Matriarchal Prehistory, 1861–1900*. University of California Press, 2011.
Engels, Friedrich. *The Origin of the Family, Private Property, and the State*. Translated by Alick West. Penguin, 2010.
Engelstein, Stefani. *Sibling Action: The Genealogical Structure of Modernity*. Columbia University Press, 2017.
Fanon, Frantz. *The Wretched of the Earth*. Translated by Constance Farrington. Penguin, 2001.
Ferris, David S. *Silent Urns: Romanticism, Hellenism, Modernity*. Stanford University Press, 2000.
Freeman, Elizabeth, ed. *Queer Kinship: Race, Sex, Belonging, Form*. Duke University Press, 2022.

Freud, Sigmund. *The Standard Edition of the Complete Psychological Works of Sigmund Freud.* 24 vols. Edited and translated by James Strachey. Hogarth Press and the Institute of Psycho-Analysis, 1953–1974.

Furet, François. *Interpreting the French Revolution.* Translated by Elborg Forster. Cambridge University Press, 1981.

Furet, François, and Mona Ozouf, eds. *A Critical Dictionary of the French Revolution.* Translated by Arthur Goldhammer. Belknap Press of Harvard University Press, 1989.

Gandhi, M. K. *The Collected Works of Mahatma Gandhi.* Vol. 8, *January–August 1908.* Publication Division, Ministry of Education and Broadcasting, Government of India, 1962.

Garcia, Tristan. *A Life Intense: A Modern Obsession.* Translated by Abigail RayAlexander, Christopher RayAlexander, and Jon Cogburn. Edinburgh University Press, 2018.

Gerould, Daniel. *Guillotine: Its Legend and Lore.* Blast, 1992.

Glick, Jeremy. *The Black Radical Tragic: Performance, Aesthetics, and the Unfinished Haitian Revolution.* New York University Press, 2016.

Goldfarb, Michael. *Emancipation: How Liberating Europe's Jews from the Ghetto Led to Revolution and Renaissance.* Scribe, 2014.

Goldhill, Simon. "Antigone and the Politics of Sisterhood." In *Laughing with Medusa: Classical Myth and Feminist Thought*, edited by Vanda Zajko and Miriam Leonard. Oxford University Press, 2006.

Goldhill, Simon. *The Christian Invention of Time: Temporality and the Literature of Late Antiquity.* Cambridge University Press, 2022.

Goldhill, Simon. "Resisting Resistance." In *Articulating Resistance Under the Roman Empire*, edited by Daniel Jolowicz and Jaś Elsner. Cambridge University Press, 2022.

Goldhill, Simon, and Robin Osborne. *Rethinking Revolutions Through Ancient Greece.* Cambridge University Press, 2006.

Güthenke, Constanze. *Feeling and Classical Philology: Knowing Antiquity in German Scholarship, 1770–1920.* Cambridge University Press, 2020.

Gutwirth, Madelyn. *Corneille's "Horace" and David's "Oath of the*

Horatii": A Chapter in the Politics of Gender in Art. Peter Lang, 2011.

Harloe, Katherine. *Winckelmann and the Invention of Antiquity: History and Aesthetics in the Age of Altertumswissenschaft*. Oxford University Press, 2013.

Hartog, François. *Anciens, modernes, sauvages*. Galaade, 2005.

Hegel, G. W. F. *Phenomenology of Spirit*. Translated by A. V. Miller. Clarendon Press, 1977.

Heine, Heinrich. *On the History of Religion and Philosophy in Germany and Other Writings*. Edited by Terry Pinkard. Translated by Howard Pollack-Milgate. Cambridge University Press, 2007.

Hobbes, Thomas. *Behemoth, or The Long Parliament*. Edited by Ferdinand Tönnies. Barnes & Noble, 1969.

Honig, Bonnie. *Antigone Interrupted*. Cambridge University Press, 2013.

Honig, Bonnie. *A Feminist Theory of Refusal*. Harvard University Press, 2021.

Hunt, Lynn. *The Family Romance of the French Revolution*. University of California Press, 1997.

James, C. L. R. *Notes on Dialectics: Hegel, Marx, Lenin*. Allison and Busby, 1980.

James, C. L. R. *The Black Jacobins: Toussaint L'Ouverture and the San Domingo Revolution*. Vintage, 1989.

James, C. L. R. *American Civilization*. Edited by Anna Grimshaw and Keith Hart. Blackwell, 1993.

Jolowicz, Daniel, and Jas Elsner, eds. *Articulating Resistance Under the Roman Empire*. Cambridge University Press, 2022.

Kant, Immanuel. *The Conflict of the Faculties*. Translated by Mary Gregor. Abaris, 1979.

Kant, Immanuel. *Political Writings*. Edited by H. S. Reiss. Translated by H. B. Nisbet. Cambridge University Press, 1991.

Kearney, Richard. *Debates in Continental Philosophy: Conversations with Contemporary Thinkers*. Manchester University Press, 1984.

Kelly, George Armstrong. "Notes on Hegel's 'Lordship and Bondage.'" In O'Neill, *Hegel's Dialectic of Desire and Recognition*.

King, Martin Luther, Jr. *Why We Can't Wait*. Harper & Row, 1964.

Koselleck, Reinhart. *Futures Past: On the Semantics of Historical*

Tribe. Translated by Keith Tribe. Columbia University Press, 2004.

Koselleck, Reinhart. *The Practice of Conceptual History: Timing History, Spacing Concepts*. Translated by Todd Samuel Presner and others. Stanford University Press, 2002.

Koselleck, Reinhart. *Vergangene Zukunft: Zur Semantik geschichtlicher Zeiten*. Suhrkamp, 1979.

Lambert, Stephen. *The Phratries of Attica*. University of Michigan, 1998.

Langerwerf, Lydia. "Universal Slave Revolts: C. L. R. James's Use of Classical Literature in *The Black Jacobins*." In *Ancient Slavery and Abolition: From Hobbes to Hollywood*, edited by Edith Hall, Richard Alston, and Justine McConnell. Oxford University Press, 2011.

Lecznar, Adam. "The Tragedy of Aimé Césaire." In *Classicisms in the Black Atlantic*, edited by Ian Moyer, Adam Lecznar, and Heidi Morse. Oxford University, 2020.

Leonard, Miriam. *Tragic Modernities*. Harvard University Press, 2015.

Loraux, Nicole. *The Divided City: On Memory and Forgetting in Ancient Athens*. Princeton University Press, 2002.

Mainz, Valerie. "Bringing the Hemlock Up: Jacques-Louis David's *Death of Socrates* and the Inventions of History." In *Socrates from Antiquity to the Enlightenment*, edited by Michael Trapp. Ashgate, 2007.

Marx, Karl. *Early Writings*. Translated and edited by T. B. Bottomore. McGraw-Hill, 1964.

Marx, Karl. *The Eighteenth Brumaire of Louis Bonaparte*. Progress Publishers, 1972.

Marx, Karl, and Friedrich Engels. *Collected Works*. Vol. 19, *1861–1864*. International Publishers, 1975.

Mazlish, Bruce. "The Tragic Farce of Marx, Hegel, and Engels: A Note." *History and Theory* 11, no. 3 (1972): 335–37.

McConnell, Justine. "Staging the Haitian Revolution in London: Britain, the West Indies and C. L. R. James's *Toussaint Louverture*." In *Greek and Roman Classics in the British Struggle for Social Reform*, edited by Henry Stead and Edith Hall. Bloomsbury Academic, 2015.

Michel, Régis, and Marie-Catherine Sahut. *David: L'art et le politique*. Gallimard, 2003.

Mitchell, Juliet. *Fratriarchy: Sibling Trauma and the Law of the Mother*. Routledge, 2023.

Möller, Astrid, and Nino Luraghi. "Time in the Writing of History: Perceptions and Structures." *Storia della storiografia* 28 (1995): 3–15.

Momigliano, Arnaldo. "Time in Ancient Historiography." *History and Theory* 6 (1966): 1–23.

Nancy, Jean-Luc. "Fraternity." Translated by Sarah Clift. *Angelaki: Journal of the Theoretical Humanities* 18, no. 3 (2013): 119–23.

Nietzsche, Friedrich. *Beyond Good and Evil*. Translated by Helen Zimmern. Wiley, 2020.

Nietzsche, Friedrich. *Untimely Meditations*. Translated by R. J. Hollingdale. Cambridge, 2012.

Oakley, S. P. "Dionysius of Halicarnassus and Livy on the Horatii and the Curiatii." In *Ancient Historiography and Its Contexts: Studies in Honour of A. J. Woodman*, edited by Christina S. Kraus, John Marincola, and Christopher Pelling. Oxford University Press, 2010.

Ober, Josiah. *The Athenian Revolution: Essays on Greek Democracy and Political Theory*. Princeton University Press, 1999.

O'Neill, John, ed. *Hegel's Dialectic of Desire and Recognition*. State University of New York Press, 1996.

Ovid. *Metamorphoses*. 6 vols. Translated by Frank Justus Miller. Revised by G. P. Goold. Loeb Classical Library 42. Harvard University Press, 1916.

Ozouf, Mona. "Fraternity." In Furet and Ozouf, *Critical Dictionary of the French Revolution*.

Paolucci, Anne, and Henry Paolucci, eds. *Hegel on Tragedy*. Harper, 1975.

Perovic, Sanja, *The Calendar in Revolutionary France: Perceptions of Time in Literature, Culture, Politics*. Cambridge University Press, 2012.

Pirro, Robert. *Hannah Arendt and the Politics of Tragedy*. Northern Illinois University Press, 2001.

Plato. *Republic*. Translated by Paul Shorey. Harvard University Press, 1969.

Plato. *Timaeus. Critias. Cleitophon. Menexenus. Epistles*. Translated by R. G. Bury. Loeb Classical Library 234. Harvard University Press, 1929.

Potts, Alex. *Flesh and the Ideal: Winckelmann and the Origins of Art History*. Yale University Press, 1994.

Prawer, S. S. *Marx and World Literature*. Clarendon Press, 1976.

Puyol, Angel. *Political Fraternity: Democracy Beyond Freedom and Equality*. Routledge, 2019.

Rabbitt, Kara. "C. L. R. James's Figuring of Toussaint-Louverture: *The Black Jacobins* and the Literary Hero." In *C. L. R. James: His Intellectual Legacies*, edited by Selwyn R. Cudjoe and William E. Cain. University of Massachusetts Press, 1995.

Ritter, Joachim. *Hegel and the French Revolution: Essays on the Philosophy of Right*. Translated by Richard Fien Winfield. MIT Press, 1984.

Roediger, David. "Accounting for the Wages of Whiteness: U.S. Marxism and the Critical History of Race." In *Wages of Whiteness and Racist Symbolic Capital*, edited by Wulf D. Hund, Jeremy Krikler, and David Roediger, 9–36. LIT, 2011

Rood, Tim, Carol Atack, and Tom Phillips. *Anachronism and Antiquity*. Bloomsbury Academic, 2020.

Rousseau, Jean-Jacques. *"The Social Contract" and Other Later Political Writings*. Edited and translated by Victor Gourevitch. Cambridge University Press, 1997.

Sala-Molins, Louis. *Le Code Noir, ou le calvaire de Canaan*. Presses Universitaires de France, 1987.

Schama, Simon. *The Power of Art*. Bodley Head, 2006.

Schama, Simon. Review of *A Palace for a King: The Buen Retiro and the Court of Philip IV*, by Jonathan Brown and J. H. Elliott. *Journal of Modern History* 53, no. 4 (1981): 683–91.

Schmitt, Carl. *Political Theology: Four Chapters on the Concept of Sovereignty*. Translated by George Schwab. University of Chicago Press, 2005.

Schwartz, Regina M. *The Curse of Cain: The Violent Legacy of Monotheism*. University of Chicago Press, 1997.

Schlegel, Friedrich. "Athenaeum Fragments." In Beiser, *Early Political Writings of the German Romantics*.

Scott, David. *Conscripts of Modernity: The Tragedy of Colonial Enlightenment*. Duke University Press, 2004.
Shapin, Steven. *The Scientific Revolution*. University of Chicago Press, 1996.
Shklar, Judith N. "Self-Sufficient Man: Dominion and Bondage." In O'Neill, *Hegel's Dialectic of Desire and Recognition*.
Sivasundaram, Sujit. *Waves Across the South: A New History of Revolution and Empire*. University of Chicago Press, 2020.
Sophocles. *Antigone. Women of Trachis. Philoctetes. Oedipus at Colonus*. Edited and translated by Hugh Lloyd-Jones. Loeb Classical Library 21. Harvard University Press, 1994.
Stallybrass, Peter. "'Well Grubbed, Old Mole': Marx, Hamlet, and the (Un)fixing of Representation." *Cultural Studies* 12, no. 1 (1998): 3–14.
Syme, Ronald. *The Roman Revolution*. Oxford University Press, 1939.
Taylor, Charles. *The Secular Age*. Belknap Press of Harvard University Press, 2007.
Toscano, Alberto. "Oneself as an Enemy: Tragedy and the Dialectic." *Crisis and Critique* 10, no. 2 (2023): 251–61.
Toscano, Alberto. "Tragedy and Jubilee." *Ethnic and Racial Studies Review* 39, no. 3 (2016): 352–59.
Vasunia, Phiroze. "Gandhi and Socrates." *African Studies* 74 (2015): 175–85.
Volney, C.-F. *Leçons d'histoire*. Edited by J. Gaulmier. Garnier, 1980.
Weineck, Silke-Maria. "The Laius Syndrome, or The Ends of Political Fatherhood." *Cultural Critique*, no. 74 (2010): 131–46.
Weineck, Silke-Maria. *The Tragedy of Fatherhood: King Laius and the Politics of Paternity in the West*. Bloomsbury Academic, 2014.
White, Hayden. *Metahistory: The Historical Imagination in Nineteenth-Century Europe*. Johns Hopkins University Press, 1973.
Whitmarsh, Tim "(Not) Talkin' 'bout a Revolution: Managing Constitutional Crisis in Athenian Political Thought." In *After the Crisis: Remembrance, Re-anchoring and Recovery in Ancient*

Greece and Rome, edited by Jacqueline Klooster and Inger N. I. Kuin. Bloomsbury Academic, 2020.

Williams, Raymond. *Keywords: A Vocabulary of Culture and Society*. Oxford University Press, 1985.

Wills, Gary. *Lincoln at Gettysburg: The Words That Remade America*. Simon & Schuster, 1993.

Wilson, Emily. *The Death of Socrates*. Harvard University Press, 2007.

Winckelmann, J. J. *Geschichte der Kunst des Alterthums*. Vienna, 1776.

Winckelmann, J. J. *History of the Art of Antiquity*. Translated by Francis Mallgrave. Getty Research Institute, 2006.

Zeitlin, Froma. "The Dynamics of Misogyny: Myth and Mythmaking in the *Oresteia*." *Arethusa* 11, no. 1/2 (1978): 149–84.

Žižek, Slavoj. *First as Tragedy, Then as Farce*. Verso, 2009.

Index

Page numbers followed by *f* refer to figures.

Aaron, 91
Abel, 91, 100
Aeschylus, 50, 73; *Oresteia*, 98–103; *Prometheus Bound*, 50, 73
Aeson, 74–76
Alcibiades, 40
Amis des Noirs (Friends of the blacks), 65–66, 120
ancien régime, 11, 50, 61, 78, 82
Antigone, 51, 92–93, 104, 109. *See also* Sophocles
Antoinette, Marie, 57–58
Apollo, 74, 76, 100, 101, 104
Arab Spring, 108
Aravamudan, Srinivas, 66, 68, 75–76
Arendt, Hannah, 69; "The Concept of History," 24–26; *On Revolution*, 1, 12, 13, 18–45, 73–74, 107–9, 110, 111
Aristotle, 1, 120; *Poetics*, 73; *Politics*, 33, 62, 87, 93
Arthur, Chris, 63–64
Aspasia, 85, 88
Athena, 85, 101, 104
Augustine, *City of God*, 25–26

Bachofen, J. J., *Das Mutterecht*, 99–102
Balzac, Honoré de, 96
Bayly, Christopher, 12, 116

Beethoven, Ninth Symphony, 89
Benjamin, Walter, 35–36, 109
Blanc, Louis, 34
Bonaparte, Louis, 52, 54, 55
Brissot, Jacques-Pierre, 65
Brooks, Peter, 55
Brutus, Lucius Junius, 7, 14–16, 36, 39, 42, 109
Buck-Morss, Susan, 61, 62, 63, 64
Burke, Edmund, 5; *Reflections on the Revolution in France*, 57–59, 119, 122

Cain, 91, 110
Catiline, 40
Caussidière, Marc, 34
Césaire, Aimé, 61, 77
Chateaubriand, François-René de, 41
Chinese Communist Revolution, 12, 16, 46
Cicero, 1
Cixous, Hélène, 102–3
Clytemnestra, 101, 106
Code Noir (Black code), 64–65
colonialism, 9–10, 65, 73–77, 97, 121
Comay, Rebecca, 17, 27, 29, 47, 58–59
comedy, 13, 47, 50–51, 54–56, 61, 69, 77, 119
Condorcet, Marquis de, 20, 65

Copernicus, Copernican Revolution, 1–2
Corneille, Pierre, 81
Crow, Thomas, 82

Danton, Georges, 34
David, Jacques-Louis, 43; *The Death of Socrates*, 5–8, 6f, 13, 117, 122; *The Intervention of the Sabine Women*, 43–44, 44f; *The Lictors Bring to Brutus the Bodies of His Sons*, 7, 14–16, 39f, 42, 109; *The Oath of the Horatii*, 7, 38–39, 79–82, 80f, 89, 96, 106; *The Tennis Court Oath*, 38, 38f
Debucourt, Philibert-Louis, 22, 23f
Declaration of Independence, 19, 97
Declaration of the Rights of Man and of the Citizen, 4, 83
democracy, 1, 8, 9, 32, 33, 37–39, 42, 55, 70, 84, 87–90, 93, 97–98, 103–4, 106, 108, 110, 125
Derrida, Jacques, 13; *The Politics of Friendship*, 86–89; *Specters of Marx*, 36, 60
Desmoulins, Camille, 59
Diderot, Denis, 5, 6, 74–77, 120, 122
Dionysius of Halicarnassus, 81
Dionysos, 74
Du Bois, W. E. B., 77

Eller, Cynthia, 101
Engels, Friedrich, 119; *Origin of the Family, Private Property, and the State*, 99–102
Engelstein, Stefani, 89–90
epic, 13, 16, 61, 77
equality, 21, 83, 85–87, 90, 91, 97, 98, 103, 104, 106
Erechtheus, 85
Eteocles, 91, 104
Euripides: *Bacchae*, 97; *Medea*, 77; *Orestes*, 104

Fanon, Frantz, 10–11
Ferris, David, 43
Fichte, Johann Gottlieb, 48–49
Foucault, Michel, 58; *Discipline and Punish*, 58–59
Freud, Sigmund, 102–5, 124; *Moses and Monotheism*, 98–99, 102; *Totem and Taboo*, 95–96, 97–98, 102
Furet, François, 11–12

Gandhi, Mohandas K., 11, 12, 13; *Story of a Soldier of Truth*, 9–11
Garcia, Tristan, 2
Glick, Jeremy, 70
Goethe, Johann Wolfgang von, 48–49, 73, 124
Goldhill, Simon, 14, 103–4
guillotine, 11, 57–59

Haitian Revolution, 14, 47, 62–77
Hartog, François, 41–42
Hebrew Bible, 91; *Exodus*, 68
Hegel, G. W. F., 34, 50–51, 54, 61, 73, 99, 108, 109, 119–20; *Aesthetics*, 51, 55, 61; *Phenomenology of Spirit*, 51, 61, 62, 63–64, 70, 93; *Philosophy of Right*, 51
Heine, Heinrich, 48–49
Heraclitus, 26
Hobbes, Thomas, 108
Homer, 3, 49, 85, 88, 118
Honig, Bonnie, 97, 124
Hunt, Lynn, 93–95

Isaac, 97

Jacobins, 41–42, 62, 66, 67, 70, 72
James, C. L. R., 13; *Black Jacobins*, 62–77, 122; *Toussaint Louverture*, 70
January 6 insurrection, 108
Jefferson, Thomas, 19

Jesus, 97
Jewish emancipation, 4–5, 16, 86
Joyce, James, *Ulysses*, 88

Kant, Immanuel: *The Conflict of the Faculties*, 47–48; "What Is Enlightenment?," 3–4, 5, 14
King, Martin Luther, Jr., 11–12
Koselleck, Reinhardt, 12, 34
Kuhn, Thomas, 2

Lenin, Vladimir, 18
Leroux, Pierre, 83
liberty, 21, 29–30, 42, 68, 83, 90
Lincoln, Abraham, 53–56, 61, 69, 77, 119
Livy, *History of Rome*, 80–82
Louis XVI (king), 14, 42, 50, 65, 79, 94, 96
Lucian, 50, 51
Luraghi, Nino, 26

Mao Zedong, 98
Marat, Jean-Paul, 14, 59, 65, 94, 95
Marcuse, Herbert, 108
Marx, Karl, 12, 13, 16, 18, 57, 59, 61, 62, 63, 73, 99, 100, 119, 121; on Abraham Lincoln, 53–56, 69, 77; *The Communist Manifesto* (with Engels), 63; *A Contribution to the Critique of Hegel's "Philosophy of Right,"* 50–51; *The Eighteenth Brumaire of Louis Bonaparte*, 15–16, 34–41, 45, 51–54, 60, 71–72, 78, 102, 108, 109, 111
Medea, 75–77, 103
melodrama, 54–56
Mendelssohn, Moses, 4–5, 14, 16
Mengs, Anton Raphael, 6
Mirabeau, Comte de, 4–5, 14, 65–66, 79, 83, 96
Mitchell, Juliet, 105–6
Möller, Astrid, 26

Momigliano, Arnaldo, 26
Morgan, Lewis H., 99
Moses, 91

Nancy, Jean-Luc, 91, 93, 103
Napoleon, Bonaparte, 21, 37, 64, 72, 98, 104, 121
National Assembly, 4, 5, 38, 120
Nietzsche, Friedrich, 46, 48–49, 51, 56, 74, 78; *The Birth of Tragedy*, 51; *Untimely Meditations*, 56

Oedipus, 30, 74, 78, 96, 97, 98, 102, 104, 105, 106; Oedipus complex, 96, 104, 105, 124. *See also* Freud, Sigmund; Sophocles
Orestes, 100, 101, 103, 104, 106
Ovid, *Metamorphoses*, 75–77
Ozouf, Mona, 44–45, 83

patricide, 95–98
Pericles, 85, 88
Perovic, Sanja, 21, 27, 114
Plato, 1, 7, 14, 16, 62, 119, 120; *Apology*, 9; *Crito*, 6; *Menexenus*, 84–85; *Phaedo*, 5; *Republic*, 32–33, 84
Plutarch, 81
Polybius, 1, 32–33
Polynices, 91, 104
postcolonialism. *See* colonialism
Potts, Alex, 42–43
Prometheus, 50, 73, 76, 77, 122
Prudhomme, Louis, 95

queer, 14, 93, 104

Raynal (abbé), 67, 72, 74–77, 122
Remus, 91, 110
Republican calendar, 13, 18, 21–28, 23f, 28f, 79, 83
Restif de la Bretonne, Nicolas, 59
Robespierre, Maximilien, 20, 29, 30, 34, 36, 37, 65, 121

Romme, Gilbert, 21
Romulus, 43, 91, 110
Rousseau, Jean-Jacques, 5, 7, 64, 82; *The Social Contract*, 64
Russian Revolution (1917), 1, 5, 12, 16

Saint-Just, Louis Antoine de, 42–43
San Domingo. *See* Haitian Revolution
Schama, Simon, 81–82, 123
Schelling, Friedrich, 30
Schiller, Friedrich, "Ode to Joy," 89–90
Schlegel, Friedrich, 49–50, 59
Schmitt, Carl, 24
Schwartz, Regina, 98, 103, 124, 125
Scott, David, 69, 73–74, 77
Scott-Heron, Gil, 46, 60
Shapin, Steven, 1
Shklar, Judith, 62
Silenus, 74
Sivasundaram, Sujit, 12, 116
slavery, 53–54, 61–66, 71–72, 120
Socrates, 5–11, 12, 14, 85, 88
Sophocles, 49, 120; *Antigone*, 51, 92–93, 104, 109; *Oedipus at Colonus*, 74; *Oedipus Tyrannus*, 30, 102

sorority, 91, 93, 104, 124, 125
Sparta, 41, 68, 108
Spartacus, 68, 121
Stalin, Joseph, 98

Tarquinius Superbus, 14
Toussaint-Louverture, 67–76
tragedy, 13, 16, 25, 29–30, 34, 47, 50–61, 68–78, 101–2, 104, 107–10
Trudaine family, 6–7
Trump, Donald, 108
Tyrtaeus, 41

Volney, Comte de, 41

Weineck, Silke-Maria, 97
White, Hayden, 46–47, 69, 77
Wilson, Emily, 8
Winckelmann, J. J., 3, 6, 8–9, 42–43
Wolf, Friedrich August, 3, 118
Wordsworth, William, 69

Xanthippe, 6

Zhou Enlai, 46
Žižek, Slavoj, 107, 108, 110

www.ingramcontent.com/pod-product-compliance
Lightning Source LLC
Chambersburg PA
CBHW022017290426
44109CB00015B/1200